A STEP AHEAD

IS BEING IN STEP WITH GEN-NEXT

NEERJA SINGH

INDIA • SINGAPORE • MALAYSIA

ISBN

Hardcase 979-8-89699-781-8
Paperback 979-8-89673-301-0

Contents

Foreword

It's a question, a feeling, that confounds most of us as we pass from one stage of life to the next: how do we stay 'in touch' across the gap of time, as the world yields to new ideas and new ways of being and doing? How do we communicate, or even understand those who are at a different phase even as we struggle to keep up with the many changes in our social, cultural, and environmental contexts? These are concerns of particular significance to those who interact with young people either in parenting or teaching/mentoring or leadership roles. As Neerja Singh so lucidly and compellingly demonstrates in her writing, there is a need to pro-actively reach across the generational divide and build bridges that are informed by an empathetic curiosity about how young people's lives today have been transformed by technology.

This book has grown out of Neerja's consistent engagement with young people, from Millennials to Zoomers, and her close observation of the many contemporary influences on their everyday lives both in and out of school. Whether it is their obsessive preoccupation with affirmation on social media and their immersion in screens, or their ways of learning about the world through the Internet, or the manner in which they construct a presence online through image and text, reimagining relationships and even work, Neerja has been asking questions and seeking answers to how we might find pathways to building these communicative bridges. Over the past several years, her column in Teacher Plus—aptly titled *A Step Ahead*—has offered insights to readers of the magazine, most of whom are teachers struggling to make some sense of our brave new world, and these new generations of children and adolescents whose lives are so enmeshed with (and within) technology.

A few decades ago, perhaps we could have dismissed the generation gap as an undeniable fact of life, or simply accepted that it could not be traversed. But given the enormous pressures young people feel today, it is important that we offer them what support we can as they navigate our uncertain times. The rise of anxiety-related disorders and other mental health stressors experienced by young people makes it crucial that we build and maintain communicative bridges. Even as we may come from a different world, there's no denying that we now occupy a shared era, nor can we argue that understanding is impossible. This is where Neerja's work offers hope, giving us a way to stay 'a step ahead'.

As editor of Teacher Plus, I've learned so much from Neerja's pieces, infused as they are with practical advice and pointed observations, and am so happy that this book will take those words to a larger audience.

– Dr Usha Raman
Editor Teacher Plus Magazine
Professor Department of Communication,
University of Hyderabad

The Witch Renaissance

Remember "Sabrina the Teenage Witch"? An American TV sitcom based on the Archie Comics that premiered in 1996?

Who would have known that the wickedly funny and recklessly brave Sabrina would herald the Witch Renaissance we are seeing today?

Our GenNext girls are turning to occult, they are pouring over astrology, crystals and tarot. Are the educationists, policy makers and parents paying attention to the mainstreaming of "Professional Witches"?

Remember? There was a time when spell work was confined to the rural hinterland, associated with an illiterate population. The word 'witch' meant "someone who causes harm to others by mystical means." There has been a transformation since among the urban teenagers and the young. The word, witch, has come to mean someone who is "an embodiment of her truth in all its power". From wicked devil-worshippers, witches have come to be repositioned and accepted as intuitive wise women.

Consider the possible reasons. Our young feel disenfranchised in the brittle and incomprehensible world they live in. The recent events, whether the pandemic, climate related disasters or humanitarian crises in different parts of the world, have shaken the foundations of society. The older generation does not inspire confidence. Instability is on the rise in the climate, politics, economy and society. The usual channels of institutional trust and dependability do not seem to work. It is against this backdrop that the potential of tapping into unseen, unconventional sources of power can have great appeal for people who feel disenfranchised or wary of the uncertain and broken environment.

In contrast, covens present a close knit, supportive alternative to anxious teenage girls. They find it easy to breathe there, out of the shadows of repressive patriarchies. There are no established figures of authority. There is a focus on female solidarity which gives young people the courage to reclaim their personal power that is suppressed due to societal conditioning. Witchcraft also offers a vocabulary of exploration without being dogmatic and prescriptive. The community structure enables them to teach themselves alongside friends and mentors. The values of group participation, communication and experimentation are encouraged in these loose structures. Many teenagers also find the magical exercises very powerful. It is reassuring to feel that there is something else that exists beyond our physical senses.

Even though it might come across like distant reasoning, witchcraft is perhaps an understandable and logical response to the environmental devastation and gender revolution. Against the ecological despair one sees and hears today, the pagan beliefs tune into nature. They uphold values of alignment with the earth rather than abusing it to serve human needs. Witchcraft honours the elements, the changing of season, the planetary cycles. It is a culture that recognizes and celebrates connectedness. As a matter of fact, it has been described as a feminine-focused, earth-centred way of living by its practitioners, which fits in nicely with a society that has been ripe for a female dominated, nature intensive movement.

This subculture is also integrating youth, gender, creative and digital culture. The reality is that witchcraft's message of respect, when combined with its rich visual culture, makes it very suitable for social media.

You may not care much about reconnecting with the earth or your inner goddess but it may feel nice to share a few well filtered photos of pretty crystals. When ideology and iconography stop agreeing, people find release and comfort in alternate beliefs. There hasn't been a subculture lately with witchcraft's ability to leverage the web. Esoteric and occult information is readily available. Grimoires are standing in for Google. No more those trips to out of the way lanes and specialist shops. A novice can sign into sites like thehoodwitch.com to share, research and connect.

Digital witch-celebrities like @bloodmilk, @nonalimmen and @_spirits flourish on Instagram, with tens of thousands of followers, many of whom are drawn to the aesthetic more than the craft. And there is choice! You could be a sea witch, kitchen witch, influencer witch with your own recipes for moon water and potions to manifest your desires. There is the additional appeal of there being no set criteria for being a witch. What could be more compelling to a teenager than a good-looking way of personal exploration and expression?

The casting of spells, hosting of rituals and marketing of crystals is lucrative business moreover. Urban teen witches are available to do magic on a client's behalf. It is an urban practice that is reflective in a way of Vedic astrology and its related ritual remedies. There is a new found faith in one's power to "manifest." This is not to say that there are no contrary sentiments. The posturing by young girls on social media without actually practicing magic, the commodification of witchcraft and the cultural appropriation across continents are ongoing threads of dialogue, dissent and discussion.

Speaking of the history of witches, no culture in the world can claim a monopoly on witches. Humans have universally harboured a fear of the special ability of some individuals to cause misfortune and injury to another by magical means. The belief in witchcraft has been innate to being human. And the associated mores have made it flexible enough to incorporate various cultural traditions.

Despite this modern trend however, calling oneself a witch is risky even now. In some parts of the world the stakes can go as high as life and death. People fear embracing magic openly. It could involve them losing their jobs, even families. Witch-hunting is institutionalized in Saudi Arabia where witchcraft and sorcery are considered crimes punishable by death. UK's Metropolitan Police by contrast has produced a 300-page guidebook, which includes instructions on how to deal with members of the pagan community: a ‘how to arrest a witch’ guide for cops.

The question to ask would be: is this a backlash against the scientific spirit of enlightenment that brought mankind to what we call “progress” today?

Witches believe that magic is inseparable from the mundane. And that what we think normal is actually magical. Magic is not in a wand outside us, it is inside of beings that live on a blue planet, spinning slowly in the universe, afloat and accurate.

A pentagram necklace, aura photography, tarot cards and a niche app industry…the occult is having its moment.

Untreated Pandemic

A problem surfaces; science takes time to resolve it and then the rest of us take our time catching up with science. Human history has been like that. With the World Wide Web going live on 6 Aug 1991, a transformation was set in motion, the likes of which mankind could never have foreseen. Facebook came in 2004, Twitter followed in 2006 and Instagram made its debut in 2010, all in a short span of six years. Two core components of this phenomenon are affecting our children in fundamental ways today and the proof is Delhi's "Bois Locker Room" incident. It behoves the adults to ask what could have been the source of the language and imagery used on the Instachat quoted.

The ease of access and nature of content available online today may help to put this alarming incident into context. All the social media platforms sustain themselves on the advertiser supported model. For a social media site to go from 300 million users to 2.5 billion and beyond, access has to be easy, almost effortless, and most of all, free. And even though there is talk of 'breaking the law' in terms of age limits, these age limits are in fact not law. The reason that a majority of social networks have these age limits and use the magic number of 13 years, is to comply with USA's COPPA laws (Children's Online Privacy Protection Act). This states that it is illegal for companies to obtain certain information and data from any child under the age of 13 without parental consent.

Now, let's talk about the content on these highly accessible platforms. There are hooks out there, ready to garner more users. It does not even take a click. Many a young, unprepared and impressionable mind has had adult images thrust before their saucer eyes from unexpected quarters online. And since children as young as eight or nine years roam the social media, this has the potential to grow in hugely uncomfortable and challenging directions. Parents and teachers are not only unaware most of the times but totally unprepared to help.

It has been referred to as the “new drug” out there, an “untreated pandemic”. Pornography is a multi-billion dollar global industry today, with revenue anywhere from $2 billion to $90 billion per year. It is a growing, constantly evolving business with employees, revenue, taxes and publicity events. It was thanks to the internet that it went from being the taboo “magazine under the bed” motif to an immediately accessible commodity. Age no bar!

Consider the demographics for a moment. India is the youngest country in the world. As per a 2018 survey by the world’s most popular porn website Pornhub, the nation is also the third largest consumer of adult content right behind the USA and UK. And a new report reveals that 89% people in India watched porn via mobile devices in 2019. India also happens to have the world's highest data usage per smartphone at an average of 9.8 GB per month that will double to 18 GB by 2024, according to Swedish telecom equipment maker Ericsson. And although several Indian telecom operators have blocked a number of adult sites, their content can be accessed on mirror domains in this fastest growing smartphone market with an ongoing digital revolution.

Now businesses need to be constantly offering new services, a USP, a bigger bang for the buck on the internet to the customers who are spoilt for choice. It is just too easy for them to go elsewhere if your product no longer does what they want it to. Since the consumers don't *have* to wait for something, they absolutely won't. The porn industry is no different? It retains, maintains and grows its customer base by appealing to and changing with their wants and desires, whatever they may be. Foundationally, this means having a wealth of "content". In other words, there are super normal stimuli available on these sites that hold immense power over the viewer and are capable of hijacking their attention and influencing their perception. There is a distorted view about what it means to be human on the screen and depictions involve violence, degradation and dehumanization.

Given that impulse control and ethical thinking are not yet developed in young people to the level that many of these networks require, the children are cognitively, socially and emotionally, just not ready. The unfortunate message they get from porn is that you are supposed to be violent when you are intimate. Boys learn that she likes to be hit and girls grow up thinking that if he hits, she should like it. This document of a woman's humiliation is a sure shot recipe for rape. It is bound to have a ripple effect in the social context wherein people lose their ability to connect with others in real life since nothing in the physical realm can compare with what is available on the screen.

For parents, just setting a good example is therefore not good enough. They have to inform themselves, be aware, open and relevant to the confusing world their children inhabit. There are some skills, thinking, behaviours and conversations the young will most certainly need in order to take care of themselves online. How do they determine if someone is exactly who they say they are online? How do they deal with cyberbullying, with digital drama, with possible exclusion and comparison? Do they have the resilience to the odd nasty comment and know how to deal with someone's anger and prejudice? Do they have the skills to deal with a group chat gone wrong? Can they block and report and deal with unwanted attention? Do they exercise some control over the time spent online? Are they in the know of what happens to the data and images they share?

This complex thinking that is needed to make the most accurate assumptions about the connections they make and the content they devour, should be part of their education from the moment they start hanging out online. If they are using social media early, these conversations will need to happen earlier. They will need good mentoring and role modeling about what it means to be in control of their social network feeds. To be shown how to be intentional about who they are interacting with and why, to be mindful of what they are consuming and to be aware of the effects their social media feeds have on their own social and emotional wellbeing.

Every girl needs to feel safe and every boy must be able to develop the capacity to express the full range of his humanity.

References

- https://spoindia.org/india-ranks-3rd-in-terms-of-pornhub-traffic-in-2018/
- https://www.bgr.in/news/india-leads-global-porn-consumption-on-smartphones-at-89-percent-report-867042/

The Identity Expressway

The one question a growing school student will often wrestle with is, "Who am I?"

And the answer to that will come from his teen years primarily. It is an awkward, confusing and intense stage of life, a simmering limbo of sorts, the teen hangs between crucial developmental milestones. There are pulls and pushes, fundamental conflicts of interests and perceived pressures. Even though the parents are most invested, their voices begin to dim at this time as those of the friends and thought leaders and mere acquaintances take over. It stands to reason that autonomy and personal agency, considered the hallmark of adulting, will be pursued at this age with a fierce gusto.

It has always been so, in most ways. The hormones are the same, so is the acne. The voices still break, the menstruation shows up and there is the body odour. Oh, for that oily hair and the new art of shaving. But there is one crucial difference today, something no teen of yesteryear has experienced.

There is an unimaginable clamour in the teen mind of 2020. An incessant noise. The young brain is like an expressway. There is a breakneck traffic inside, zipping in different directions, the drivers are parents, friends, coaches, Instagram, school teachers, the significant other, the YouTube, even the therapist. In contrast, recall what it was like growing up in the 80s. There was either the Ambassador or the Fiat! There were the voices of the parents or the teachers, the rest either did not exist or had very little access to the thoughts and emotions of the growing young.

The teen of yesterday had less confusion about his or her identity, there weren't that many choices. The teens today juggle several faces. They present different personas to the multitude influences in their lives. They are the photogenic, fun, breezy, awesome young beings on Instagram. At home, they present conformity, preoccupation with school work and a generic normality. To their sports coaches, they are tough as nails and driven. With friends, there is thoughtfulness and a ready ear for any of their problems. There are also cliques the teens flirt with. The popular group, the pensive empath group, the Goth group. Every subculture demands a certain presentation from the vulnerable young member.

The nature of identity has clearly changed for this generation. Where in all this highway traffic is the real teenager? That is their struggle. Who is the actual person below the several levels of constructed personalities? What does the teenager feel like deep down inside? Dark and moody? Kind and loving to herself/himself or just fatigued at all the phony and plastic identities they wear for the world?

This is the time for creating their true identities, free of the cacophony around them. It is expected that they will use the tools of their times to prepare to play a productive role in the economy and society of the future. But there are silos. Teenagers today are never truly free from anxiety. They are never truly free to hear themselves think. They are never ever off the grid of expectations and comparisons and judgments. Whether they are on the phone, at school, in a gathering, doing their school work or even with family, there is the hum in the head, always on. Managing their personal identity expressway takes a lot out of them.

To avoid uncomfortable emotions, many teens listen to music on their favourite streaming platform or watch reruns of their favourite serials or numb themselves with substances. Not being able to decide who they are and the roles they want to play in the world may feel like a failure to some teens. It then becomes easier to hide under other multiple identities. And so, the young flit from time on phone to time with family, both instances being anxiety provoking.

The first thing for a parent or teacher is to understand what is going on here. A teen's brain is not cognitively developed yet, therefore the impulsiveness in their behaviour. There is a struggle to feel unique as well as to fit in at the same time. Perhaps they feel left out or ignored because of their ethnic, gender or sexual identity. It could be that there is a lack of attachment to the parents or an absence of adult influence. Perhaps the teen does not feel accepted in a positive group of peers.

The resultant behaviour could include an unrealistic perception of oneself or promiscuous behaviour or dramatic conduct or self-recrimination. There may be intense feelings of anger or sadness. Disregarding rules and limits and boundaries, glancing around to monitor others could all be signs of a struggle to form an identity.

Now how does a parent help with all this traffic their teen is trying to negotiate? By not adding their own voice. By letting the teen hear more of his or her own voice. By staying curious. By asking open questions. By being the quiet and calm parking space into which the teens can pull up and consider themselves. By not starting to remind them of their strengths! By not trying to make them feel better! By just gentle asking and a whole lot of listening. The teens already have all the answers. Perhaps they feel lonely. Perhaps they don't value themselves all that much. Perhaps they will look at your pet dog and say, "I want that life!"

The calm, confident and safe holding space adults can provide the young today is the best thing to do. It can ease and cure and soothe frayed nerves, it is invaluable and essential for their well-being. Be quiet adults. Respect the angst the young wrestle with. There is very little point telling them what it used to be or can be. They have known nothing else other than what they live with. So, stick around and be useful while they work it out themselves with your coolness for company.

The trick is to let them go when you have the strongest urge to protect them the most.

The Hacker University

A hacker university is selling cybercrime courses designed to hack for profit and commit fraud. Known by the name HackTown, it prepares and equips professional cybercriminals. It promises the knowledge and skills needed to hack an individual or company successfully. Little or no coding experience is required of the applicants.

The rise of this university carries the rapid professionalization of cybercriminal organizations one step further. It also demonstrates that just as in the field of cybersecurity, there are skills gap that are being sought to fill up by cybercrime leaders. This presents a threat to careers in legitimate cybersecurity.

HackTown begins by offering a few free courses that cover everything from operational security to network attacks, Wi-Fi hacking and carding. It then opens the lid on further training for a fee. These range from skills for accessing router admin panels, discovering targets inside a compromised network, brute force attacks, man-in-the-middle attacks and so on.

The university holds out the promise of fast tracking the trainee's cybercriminal hacker career. An excellent staff, support and assistance for course progression are offered. HackTown ensures the students will be able to use their new-found skills to deploy ransomware and remote access trojans (RATs) for personal profit. A resource shop is being developed moreover for sale of malware, keyloggers, and password stealers needed as tools of their trade.

It ought to surprise and shock that there is an underground cybercrime training and recruitment push. Reason says otherwise. The initiatives are simply mirroring the drive of the security community to provide greater access to cyber careers. It ought not to happen though, that cybercrime becomes more appealing and within reach. In floundering economies, there is a real danger of cybercrime winning over a career in legitimate cybersecurity.

Young adults and teenagers are a target market for hacker universities. The idea is to have them become part of cybercrime activities in the roles of money mules and social engineering calls. Those tempted need to be aware of the motivations of the cybercriminals who by nature would like to maximize their success while minimizing their exposure. These universities would appear easy grounds to recruit pawns who can take the fall for them.

Just as the global universities began to teach remotely, the cybercriminals jumped on, their task made easier with straightforward payment systems and content access such as exploits and proof of concept code. YouTube is crawling with beginner level hacker information anyway, all that is needed is a pair of young, restless and idle hands on the keyboard. And even though, this is a game of earning mailbox money and advertising malware and tools, the threat of destruction is real. Several database breaches have been the result of user-friendly tooling and online guides to means of identifying vulnerabilities.

At this time, the modern cybercrime industry is ahead in organizational efficiency. The reason? Unlike cyber start-ups that keep receiving venture funding even when losing money, the cybercriminals do not have the luxury of making mistakes. But what precisely is ethical hacking? It is an authorized attempt to gain unauthorized access to a computer system, an application, or data. An ethical hack duplicates the ways and means of malicious attackers. It is an anticipatory practice to identify security vulnerabilities that can be resolved before being exploited.

The ethical hackers, also known as "white hats" carry out assessments that are diametrically opposed to those carried out by the malicious hackers. They stay legal, respect the approved boundaries, report the vulnerabilities along with remedial advice and are committed to non-disclosure. In contrast to the cybercriminals, ethical hackers use their expertise to secure and improve organizational technology. Their service is essential to preventing security breaches. Malicious hackers on the other hand, will deface websites, crash backend servers, cause damage to reputation and financial loss.

Some of the most common vulnerabilities ethical hackers find are injection attacks, broken authentication, security misconfigurations, sensitive data exposure and use of components with known vulnerabilities. There are limitations to ethical hacking however. The scope, resource constraints of time, computing power, budget and denial of test cases that can lead to server crash hold back the White Hats many a time.

The new wave of cyberattackers from Generation Z (born 1996 to 2012) are concentrating on Discord, the gaming chat service. They work behind the scenes to both infiltrate organizations as well as prevent others from doing it. These hackers are younger, their access to resources is more which makes them far more formidable than those gone before. Social media platforms such as Discord and Telegram are the stealth hotbed for them through which they can spread extremely sophisticated ransomware and malware with little chance of being caught.

Cybersecurity and a seamless protection have become critical in the hyper-distributed era of work-from-home where everyone is distanced, mobile and unsecure. The exposure points are too many given the cloud-enabled workforces.

What can the regular folks do to protect themselves? The oldest and simplest computer fix to keep hackers off track is to turn a device off and then back on again. Phones have become digital souls for users. They are always within reach; they are rarely turned off and they hold huge stores of personal and sensitive data. It is little wonder therefore that they are top targets for hackers looking to steal text messages, contacts, photos, locations. At a time of widespread digital insecurity, rebooting phones will not stop the cybercriminals completely but will make them work harder. It imposes cost on the malicious mischief-makers. For this reason, it is recommended that the phone be rebooted every week.

This advice stems from the rise of a new technology hackers use today to break into mobile devices. Called the “zero-click” exploits, they do not need the user to open any shady link that is secretly infected. Once access is gained, the hacker will instal malicious software to a computer’s root file system so as to be able to stick around. Fortunately for the uninitiated and hapless users, phone manufacturers such as Apple and Google protect their core operating system with strong malware resistant security protocols.

But technology is an ongoing race. It is a matter of time before Hacker University’s students graduate from hacking systems to hacking people, then the planet.

Teen Activism

We ask our primary school students to save the earth and not burst crackers on Diwali to encourage their social sensitivity. When the same children turn teens and want to participate in the Shaheen Bagh protests or use social media to speak up for the rights of the transgender people, we tell them, "That's not your job, just study and get into a good college!" In college, some of them continue to suffer pangs of conscience but there is no role model to follow. Come graduation and the young adults enter the workforce and the desire for change begins to die down. They end up adulting like the generations gone before. And the deeply embedded injustices in society continue, no one has the time to analyze and challenge them.

Quite surprisingly, India has a rich tradition of youth movements, nonetheless. And today, when one in five young people suffer from mental illness, there has never been a greater time for generational empathy with the young throwing the gauntlet, when they do. In other words, when a teen takes to Instagram to create awareness about a social issue, rather than scoff at the armchair activism, he or she deserves adult support and encouragement. They cannot be prepared to inherit the earth when they are so grossly underrepresented in the political process across nations. If they are to come out of their present political apathy and disenchantment, they need support to participate in social justice so that parliaments begin to cater to their interests and concerns.

The young are increasingly impatient with the older generation being just inert with hopelessness. A growing number of teenage activists are taking matters into their own hands. These angry voices speak through social media and they may not be dismissed any more. The time for surprise and shock to hear teens being politically articulate is over. Believe it or not, there are teens today who ask what is the point in attending school when the earth's capacity to nurture life is falling apart. They would rather sue governments for inaction and push policy reforms. Law actions, civil disobedience, name it and the young are in the thick of it.

It is all moving younger. Not just coding but the fight for fairness to all. This Instagram link for instance https://www.instagram.com/youactproject/?hl=en works on "sparking teens into policy advocacy." Consider some cases making the headlines today. Marley Dias, 14 founded #1000blackgirlbooks campaign when she was 11 in 2015. She said she was sick of reading about white boys and dogs and decided to donate 1000 books to her peers that featured black girls as the main characters. The campaign was a massive success, and she's since been honoured on the Forbes Under 30 list. Her mission is to help youth to "open up to people who are different, to understand and to see and grow from those things we don't understand."

'Desmond is Amazing', 12, is committed to garner LGBTQ (Lesbian, gay, bisexual, and transgender) youth visibility. He performs to inspire fellow tweens and adults to "be yourself always, no matter what". Mari Copeny, 11, wrote a letter to President Barack Obama in March 2016 about the water crisis in Flint, Michigan. Obama responded to her letter and flew to Flint which put the crisis in a national spotlight. These teen activists and others like them have not just created awareness, they have followed it up with concrete action.

Not only do these teens educate their friends and family about important social causes, a growing number take personal action to live more sustainably. They donate and volunteer time to issues that interest them. I know some who have boycotted companies completely because they do not resonate with their values. My daughter does not buy from Amazon! It is teens worldwide that are holding companies responsible for their actions. Corporate social activism is a by-product of teen expectations of businesses. The message is loud and clear. Individuals and the government have the primary responsibility of "cleaning up" yes, but the young are more likely to purchase products from companies that support causes.

Teens are more in touch with the wrongs that need to be righted in the new world. So, if your teen is voicing concern about the state of things, if they are bringing in stray animals, if they are asking you to fund your domestic help's education, if they insist that you use your influence to speak in favour of the weak…stop and listen. This is a sign of hope for us all. For the woke teens, it is not just about money and fame and the fairy tale life. It is about changing something and challenging the status quo. The teens have a strong sense of fairness.

But here is the paradox. The average age of the Indian population is 27 years and that of the Indian MP is 57. The age difference is of more than a generation. It is the young that are the “excluded majority” today even though they are the cohort that have pushed increasing education, globalization and digitalization of the world. Their concerns are gender equality, climate change, poverty, unemployment, over-population while the traditionalists are still struggling with the ancient issues of casteism and religious intolerance. Many find the adult world disconnected, non-committal and disrespectful. While adults pontificate on TV panels, it is the teens mobilizing on topical issues. They deserve respect.

Youth quotas in parliaments and lowering of eligibility age ought to be considered. The young have been ridiculed for lazy, mouse click activism but the war of ideas is being fought on bandwidths, not so much on the streets anymore. WhatsApp and Instagram are routinely dismissed and trashed but that is where mental shifts are happening. Therefore, full marks to a teen who is using these to push a message of positive change rather than sharing just filtered food photos and dance videos!

There is tremendous pressure on young people today to challenge things adults should be addressing.

“When the whole world is silent, even one voice becomes powerful,” Malala Yousafzai.

Tackling Thoughts of Self-harm

It is staring us in the face today, this alarming new frontier that our kids seem to face. A quick search on the internet will throw up the disturbing new trend of self-harm and suicide among the young. According to the latest available data from the National Crime Records Bureau, a student commits suicide every hour in India. The world's second most populous country of over 1 billion has one of the highest suicide rates among those aged 15 to 29.

The suicides begin in school; continue in college and into the late 20s. Academic stress, highly competitive admissions to prestigious institutions and the whimsical job market are all contributing factors. Add to this the fear of disappointing their ambitious parents and falling behind their peers. Ironically enough, even those students who eventually do pass the entrance exams feel even more pressure to excel at university, often taking their own lives when it all becomes too much.

What is going on here? Do we have an inkling of what it is like to be in the shoes our children wear today? For instance, do parents and teachers realize that suicidal thoughts are becoming increasingly ordinary and pedestrian among young people? Kids today talk with one another, rather freely, about their thoughts of hopelessness and suicidal ideation. At times there may be a vision of plans, they might even think of how people might react once they are gone?

What were we like in contrast? There was much less self-awareness, less insecurity, and fewer comparisons to others. Who cared at age eight or nine whether other kids were smarter, more athletic, better looking, and so on? There was protection from these painful comparisons and insecurities by way of distractions and buffers that cloaked us in a cottony cocoon.

Kids today are exposed to the stimuli that fuel these comparisons every single day. It is right there, in their pocket or close by, waiting to remind them of their "imperfections," real or merely perceived. Imagine this diminishing of their minds, bodies and social capital entering the consciousness as a constant flux, the terrifying notion that they are not good enough, that they may be unloved or worse, unlovable.

Dr. Harish Shetty, a psychiatrist at Dr. L. H. Hiranandani Hospital believes that an inability to cope with small frustrations, failure and loss, often coupled with social alienation can prove critical for some students. Neerja Birla, the founder and chairperson of Mpower, a mental health organization, rightly points out that when it comes to mental health, Indian parents need to stop going into denial mode and issuing defensive statements like, "My child has no such problems!"

A survey by the Centre for the Study of Developing Societies* reveals about four in ten students in India have experienced bouts of depression in the last few years. Schools and colleges are inept at dealing with nervous breakdowns among students. They do not yet foster a culture of understanding and trust, empathy and compassion.

As parents therefore, we can no longer avoid the discussion of suicide and suicidal ideation with our children. There is more than one set of grieving parents out there who were wholly blindsided, unaware that suicide was even a thought in their child's mind. Most parents, quite understandably, will have fears that children will be suggestible, somehow, if we introduce the idea of suicide to them, that we might be planting the seed of an idea.

Historically, there may have been a time when this was the case, and parents could protect children from that degree of hopelessness. Sadly, that time is quite long gone.

Knowing she has someone to talk with, someone who is open, non-judgmental and not too afraid, is precisely what the teen suffering suicidal thoughts most needs. A safety plan can be enormously comforting too. No suicidal person truly wants to die. Most have been known to describe a "suicidal fog" in which all feels lost and hopeless. Providing them an option, a "call me without reservation," tends to allow for just enough hope to provide a beacon through the fog, one that can be truly lifesaving.

There is a new quasi-suicidal thinking afoot, the idea that "I am not going to do anything to hurt myself, but I don't care if I wake up tomorrow, either." We need to be alert, and ask "Does this have to do with the way you feel about yourself? The world? The future?" Consider too: Is your child quieter than she used to be? Is she spending more time alone? Is she down and sullen? Has her behaviour shifted dramatically? Does she suddenly seem buoyant and relieved after a period of depression? Any and all of these can be indications of suicide risk, with many more precipitants, of course. That "suicide fog" can sweep over a child in the wake of a bad test score, or fear of a disciplinary issue, or an aftermath of a sudden breakup. So, ask if she is okay and be receptive to the answer, especially if it is a no.

The bottom line is this: we are losing far too many young people to suicide – bright, talented, beautiful young people who cannot see past the moment. We can no longer keep this issue under wraps, vaguely cloaked in shame. The world our children are growing up in is a far harsher place than the one we came of age in. The right thing to do therefore is to balance the harsh messages our children receiveconstantly with gentleness. They need to know, now more than ever, that they have a soft, available place to fall.

What will be your course of action therefore if your tween does happen to be suicidal? Should your child express that she is overtly suicidal in the moment that you ask, the immediate plan would be to call a suicide prevention helpline or get to one such centre should there be trouble connecting. This will ensure her safety right away and there will be professionals for guidance through the next steps. If your child expresses some degree of suicidal ideation, but she does not have a plan and clearly is no immediate threat to herself, the thing to do would be to seek a psychologist or licensed clinical social worker, with specific experience working with young people who have experienced this despair.

It is a mighty parent that has the presence of mind to use all of the tools at her disposal to help her child regain a sense of safety and well-being. Whatever it takes!

*The findings of the 2016 Lokniti-CSDS Youth Survey indicate that around four out of 10 youngsters who are currently studying felt regular or occasional depression/tension during last couple of years. Loneliness may be one reason as in the survey 30% also confirmed feeling lonely at times.

https://www.lokniti.org/media/upload_files/KeyfindingsfromtheYouthStudy.pdf

Sadfishing

The mind seems to have been overtaken by the heart in every aspect of modern life but in an ambivalent way. Thought leaders, CEOs, *gyangurus*, life coaches…everyone claims the significance of feelings while upholding logic and reason. What are these mixed messages doing to our teenagers?

They have taken to sadfishing with the help of social media.

Have you heard of the term? It has been around since the advent of tweets, Facebook status updates and Instagram captions but most adults are unaware of the social phenomenon. Sadfishing refers to young people fishing for emotional support online by exaggerating their suffering. Sadfishing looks like posts that say, "There is too much sadness and I can't take it anymore" or that "I am ready to just give up." It attracts immediate sympathy and attention from the audience. In time, the sadness, hopelessness and negativity grow to become a toxic echo chamber that imprisons the venting teenager.

Why does a teen sadfish? It is much easier for a 14-year-old to share her struggles online in an anonymous manner with next to nil likelihood of being confronted. It is more difficult to approach someone in real life and ask for help.

A sadfishing teen may post fabricated emotional struggles that refer to mental states of anxiety, depression, even suicidal thoughts but the goal is to get attention and not necessarily genuine help. There may be sharing of some particularly negative song lyrics, young people at times will post selfies of themselves crying, there might even be a status update on how they feel the world will not miss them much.

What should a parent do under these circumstances? It is important to spell out ground rules for social media use at home. Ideally parents ought to follow their teens on the various platforms including their "finsta" or other Instagram accounts. There are parent control monitoring apps available that will alert you whenever your teen opens a new social media account. It sounds undemocratic and repressive but there are serious threats to the lives and mental health of our teens online in these hyperconnected times.

Teens post about their emotions and dark feelings with an expectation of empathy or attention or reassurance. This strategy can sometimes backfire because there are bullies out there who may manipulate the children. It is important therefore to offer compassion to your child and encourage them to share with family and friends instead. The parent or teacher must be a child's go-to person and not a stranger online.

A distasteful phenomenon of "kids grooming" happens online wherein unscrupulous adults offer support, attention and then gain the trust of emotionally expressive teens. It is therefore alright for parents to know what apps their teens are using. It is a safe practice to know what the young are doing online and who they are talking to. How does one judge, however, if it is just sadfishing or a genuine cry for help? Does the teen's behaviour offline match the online post? If it doesn't, then the anomaly ought to be nipped in the bud. In a wholesome and kind way.

A constant and ongoing conversation about safe and healthy digital activity needs to take place in homes. Adults do need to monitor their child's behaviour both online and in real life. Freaking out and meting out punishment will not work however. Your teen needs to know that they can come to you when they are in trouble.

Many teenagers claim they can be more authentic online, the level of intimacy and connectedness to their fellow users being such. Given the red flags, however, perhaps alternative outlets can be provided for validation without the negative consequences of social media-based disclosures.

So now you know your teen is sadfishing? The first thing to do is to communicate that you care deeply for them and want to support them. Establish that connection right away. Explain that there is always an option of speaking to a third person such as a school counsellor or a therapist should the teen be wary of sharing all of it with the parent. It is also important to remember that no matter how self-serving a post may appear, there well may be a grain of truth to the message.

Truth be told, social media is not a safe place for teens to regularly air their feelings or compare themselves to others. Because so many teens are sharing their raw and sometimes exaggerated feelings online, sadfishing can turn into a circus along "The Boy Who Cried Wolf." Readers start to roll their eyes when they see posts about depression and anxiety rather than offer help that may be needed. It does not help to romanticize or capitalize difficult life experiences.

Sadfishing can turn social media into an unsafe and morbid space with fatalistic expressions. It blurs the line between exaggerating emotions and becoming sucked into them, there is a real and present possibility of the vocabulary triggering mental health issues.

Whether or not a child has a Finsta, "a secret Instagram account where they express more personal thoughts", a lot more conversations need to happen around sadfishing in general. If nothing else, it will encourage your young to come to you should they feel out of sorts. They may also learn how to react to a friend who is sadfishing.

It is important to spread awareness and accountability on social media. A lot of poison flies under the radar simply because the coordinates and frequencies are unfamiliar.

As adults that are heavily invested in the young, here is an opportunity to orchestrate the right interventions so as to build stronger connections with them. We can no longer afford to miss out on this one, you never know when this support might be called in to save a precious and promising young life today.

Looking Good Can Be Bad

It has been a generation now of the "self-esteem building in children" movement. Schools, parents, institutions have raised those born roughly between 1982 and 2002 to believe that they are pearls in the oysters of the world. This cohort was told they could be anything they wanted to be simply if they put their minds to it. They grew up believing they were special and destined for greatness. They internalized all the eager adulation to take on an aura of "I could be President of India if I liked but it is not my cup of tea". And what has been the outcome? Take a look around.

Self-belief seems to touch delusional levels in some children. They have grown up thinking they can do no wrong. Their parents have been so fearful of negative outcomes, they have overextended themselves on providing their offspring daily affirmation. So petrified are we of all the talk of anxiety induced by competition that we hasten to tell them, "You are enough as you are." But what is apparently received instead is, "I just need to exist."

It sounds a bit harsh but consider what we are seeing. Boredom is anathema. Criticism is personal attack. Perseverance is a compromise. Life has to be gold dust every moment. There is no calming these restless products of an over-zealous and fearful nurturing. Look at the acronyms that define their beliefs. YOLO or you only live once. FOMO or the fear of missing out. Words like industry, struggle, fruits of labour, patience have been replaced with ikigai, every sparking moment, celebrate yourself, self-love. Even bouncing may not be backward, it has to read bouncing forward!

What's wrong however with having children feel good about themselves, one ought to ask. Is it not about them acquiring a strong core and a robust sense of identity? So long as their self-concepts are based on productive and functional behaviour and genuine, demonstrable accomplishment, it is all good. The problem arises when their self-image is falsely inflated and does not find reflection in personal, social or academic success.

And that is odd since it has been believed for long that it is in fact low self-esteem that is destructive and high-risk. Academic failure, substance abuse, promiscuity have all been typically attributed to a sense of inferiority. But there is new research now to say that a low self-esteem may not after all be that destructive. In fact, it is a high self-esteem that can lead to problematic behaviour at times. Self-absorbed, entitled and irresponsible children can be traced back to sky high praises. It has been found that many criminals and drug abusers and bullies see themselves as superior to others around them.

"The common-sense understanding of self-esteem has been obscured by its over-application," says Allan Josephson, MD, chairman of the Family Committee of the American Association of Child and Adolescent Psychiatry. "Self-esteem certainly is important. But we've developed this misguided notion that parents should continually reward and praise their children. That doesn't work either." According to him, children are more likely to act selfishly if they are either undervalued or overvalued. Those who depend on outside praise to feel good about themselves tend to struggle later in life when teachers, employers and friends do not shower them with compliments.

Has good parenting/teaching gone bad? How does one strike a balance between tough love and enabling bad behaviour? What does the middle ground look like? Perhaps the problem is not high self-esteem but false self-esteem.

There is greater integrity in praising only the noteworthy accomplishments and behaviours. It is recommended that praise be directed at the effort and not just the end result. Keep it real, in other words.

Pep talks rarely work. Despite what the life coaches tell us, we don't have to love ourselves. It keeps us from adopting practical coping strategies that succeed. As a matter of fact, some strategies to protect one's high self-esteem may include lying, hiding mistakes, making excuses, blaming others, being angry at criticism or avoiding challenges altogether. Kids with low self-esteem on the other hand may dismiss or discount their victories too. Looking good could feel bad and threatening to them because it brings focus to an "an inevitable future failure".

Low self-esteem, in addition, has been known to be emotionally painful. It can set up the child for depression and eating disorders. Children develop self-respect when they get to challenge themselves. Rather than rescue them when the going gets tough, it strengthens them to have to keep trying and figure the way out themselves. It is crucial that they understand that everyone has pluses and minuses and that it is quite normal. Being matter of fact about mistakes and not overthinking helps them to stand up again from the occasional fall life may bring. They say the mightiest adults are those the young can be at their worst with. The young benefit from knowing that no matter what, they are cherished. Social connections and their ability to empathize are sure to boost true self-esteem. Realistic expectations and a healthy respect for the young one's unique talents are other ways to help them craft a healthy sense of identity.

And enduring health more and more seems to involve moving beyond intense self-focus.

Real esteem perhaps is not about feeling special or wonderful but in letting go of the question, "Am I good enough?" It is only when the children are not judging themselves that they can be in the moment to listen and learn and grow. The way forward therefore is to let go of harsh self-evaluations. What matters more is that the three fundamental needs of connection, competence and choice be taken care of. Helping children connect with something bigger than themselves can ease the self-focus that causes low self-esteem.

So deep-seated is the bug of exclusivity today that just being ordinary and content, satisfied and satiated, restful and rested has become extraordinary. This is not to say that the self-esteem movement has been a complete waste. It just ought to be a by-product of a wholesome relationship with a child and not the goal.

It's Time…to Talk About It!

The repeated headlines about rape talk over group chat, most recently, in a Mumbai private school should come as no surprise. The manner in which the affected parties handled it was also to be expected given our record as a hide-bound society. The psychiatrists are upon the scene with their talk of "nipping it in the bud", the parents are in a state of silent shock and the authorities have washed their hands of the mess by suspending the students. Perhaps we should have talked to the boys instead, both before as well as after.

Why do we make a religion of bolting the stable door after the horse has made off? As a culture, we do not anticipate the curves ahead. Our ears are cocked at the neighbours or the screaming news anchors but not to the ground as they should be. It ought to be our mandate as the nurturers of the next generation to plot the dots and run ahead of catastrophe. It is not a skill we have learnt to value – yet. Do several more young lives need to be lost before we sit up and get our act together?

The unfortunate truth is that our children are keenly aware of the nature and pervasiveness of sexual assault in our culture. We should have begun discussing it openly with them along with sex and sexual identity a long time ago. Even though not only girls, but boys and young men are also sexually assaulted, the perpetrator is invariably a boy or a man. At the core is the idea of consent. This discussion around what constitutes consent ought to be followed by a game plan to face the reality. What should a young person do should they ever fall into a situation that feels unsafe or compromising? And can they come to us, to you and me, in the wake of sexual assault?

But is it enough to simply begin talking and practicing prevention? There has to be talk of consent, respect and behaviour of course, but it is crucial also to gauge what teenage boys think about the cause and effect of assault. Do they know what the boundaries are? Do they understand what defines sexual assault? Do they appreciate its impact on the victim? Do they have suggestions on how to prevent it?

With new definitions of sexuality and masculinity, there is a sense of insecurity, shame and confusion amongst many boys. Movements such as those of women empowerment and #MeToo have blurred the notions of what it is to be male in these times. There is a lot out there in the public domain about 'toxic masculinity' but who is outlining 'positive masculinity'?

It is a common misconception that assault is about sex. It is not. It is about power, conquest and proving oneself a "man". Often these unwelcome actions are prompted by a sense of self-loathing. It is time we begin speaking of maleness in terms of kindness, self-reliance, and respect for women, courage and a sense of humor. The current discourse about men being a blight on the culture or predators whose dark and damaging impulses need to be reined in is dangerous and utterly self-defeating.

As a society we have a lot to answer for. The disturbing and heartrending news stories are an indictment of the blinkers we refuse to take off. It is a comment on our delusional inertia that prevents us from keeping pace with our growing children. The onus is on us adults to stay on top of trends and technology. It is no longer enough to provide for their basic needs, the demand is from us to be their guides and allies and safe spaces.

We could take a few steps right off with reference to sexual assault. The first thing to do would be to stay mindful of our own language and attitudes towards gender stereotypes at home. The next wise step would be to take the mystery out of 'taboo topics' by making them a part of the family's regular conversation at home. For this, parents and educators themselves need to be well-informed and current with the prevailing trends and attitudes. The third thing to do is to literally get into the trenches with the young. 'I don't need to know' is not an option any more. It would strengthen the mutual connection if parents made an effort to engage with their music and the online content their children are consuming. The young need to know that their parents are plugged into the modern ecosystem. It is as important not to operate from a place of fear and anxiety as it is to not make harsh judgments on the perceived poor choices of our children. The very nature of society and environment has changed. It is not as linear and programmed as it was when we were teenagers. The final measure would be to throw open your home and heart to their friends irrespective of our opinion of them. When the chips are down, it boils down to open channels of communication.

This is our opportunity to help prevent sexual violence. We cannot afford not to use it and use it well. This generation is poised to carry a very different mantle. Even though we are leaving them a harsher world it is they who are forward thinking and have the potential to develop a deeper sense of humanity. The idea of the "conquest" of women and boasting of the number they have hooked up with no longer appeals to many young boys, for instance. The cultural spiel about and sanction of a male's raging hormones does not wash any more. We need to acknowledge and support these notions as much as allay the fear and anxiety in potential victims. A phenomenal personal and cultural shift hangs in the balance. Precious young lives are at stake. We better stem this tide by staying ahead of the curve.

How Relevant are Schools Today?

First there was the digital landscape and now it is Covid 19. Are schools all set to disappear to make way for a new template better suited to the needs of this era? There has been quite a buzz lately around the new phenomena of school refusal and home schooling for one.

Other, bigger questions are picking up volume. Are schools outdated today? Is school the same as education? Is Internet not capable of providing knowledge and skills? Why is education equated with a learning and teaching process that takes place in an institute when it actually is about learning anything in life?

Education is usually equated with school education, a structured way to provide the skills of literacy, language and mathematics to the masses. But what happens beyond these essential skills? Rather than continue to be about learning, it stops at schooling which is more about school buses, administrators, budgets, dress codes, rules and orders, buildings, etc.

The two factors that encourage learning – curiosity and a pro-active search for information – are rarely cultivated in the classroom. Schools are beneficial in many ways, that is not to be discounted. They provide a safe environment where children learn academics and essential life lessons and develop their talents and explore various fields. Teachers are like second parents and there are the friends that add to the fun.

However, more significant than any of these is the certification role that schools play today. And that stamp is beginning to lose value given digital technology and the Internet. Everyone has the same access to tools and information. In the information revolution, it is abundantly clear today that while the schools were designed for one thing, they are now required to deliver something else.

The classroom today for instance looks no different from the classroom of 1890. The employment horizon has transformed in fundamental ways, but schools continue to educate students for jobs that do not exist anymore. In fact, most of the syllabi is outdated. The books are rarely updated and nor is an attempt made to refresh material with supplements from the Internet and additional reading. As a matter of fact, most of the regular work done by students in the classrooms is low-end cognitive work while out in the labour force, skills that are required are largely creative thinking and collaboration,which in turn are based on cognitive, non-routine tasks.

How about the "flipped classroom model"? A student watches a short video on a math concept, she solves some examples herself and then takes them to the teacher for feedback and inputs. Leveraged and fine-tuned enough, technology can transform the teaching-learning experience for both the teacher and the taught. What is happening instead is transference of a system on how to be an employee and obey. A student that writes precisely as is expected of her in an exam will grow to be the subordinate who will do only as much is demanded of her by the boss, no extra initiative, no taking ownership.

What we are seeing around us is the greatest, deepest, most rapid expansion of human expression in all of human history. Nobody need be stuck to a writing table or an office anymore. That device in the pocket can do it all. But schools continue to perpetrate and cultivate a consumer mindset rather than a creative one. The Internet, for instance, is a place where we pull down some content put up by another. It is, in fact, a highly participatory space, social and interactive. It is a landscape to be doing in and making and creating upon. What is taking the schools so long to realize this?

In today's world where everyone has a voice, it is tragic that schools do so little with the normative sciences that will give students a unique world view. Just the subject matter and homework leaves the students little time for personal growth of any other nature. With most knowledge having been committed to memory; students feel lost after school. There have been only exams that are focused on results, nothing resembling continuous learning. At that tender age, it is not unheard of some young children going astray or having been so affected by favouritism at the hand of teachers that they grow up feeling worthless and incompetent.

In the current wake of the pandemic, WHO declares India as the most depressed country in the world. One in six children and teenagers between 10-19 years of age suffer from depression. There is said to be one suicide attempt every three seconds and one death by suicide every 40 seconds by our youth.* School education clearly causes a whole lot of stress in students who seem unable to cope with pressure from parents and teachers to excel at studies. One major reason for this is also the fact that the children's emotional and social development is ignored by the educators. The theme song remains "survival of the fittest" and the young minds are brought up to be competitive from their earliest years. It is quite common for Indian parents to flaunt the marksheet of their child. But what about those who are not able to score well in exams? There are feelings of frustration, depression, anger, sorrow and acute resentment at times with no skills to manage them.

Ideally, the school ought to focus on growing and strengthening the personal and problem-solving skill of their students. How wonderful it would be if students did not feel forced into subjects and instead could explore several possibilities. Practical and professional skill-based education would help the students be clearer on their career goals.

It is possible today to thrive in communities of mutual interest rather than just geography. Rather than teach them to regurgitate, schools ought to prepare students to be adaptive. But the bigger picture is not something school leadership is looking at. Perhaps it is parents too who need to unlearn their experiences of school which fashions their expectations of the teachers and principals.

This is the time for uncomfortable conversations on how the world has changed, the transformation in education and what our children will face when they leave the main gate of their schools. Teaching has to be for growth. Education has to address the employment sectors. It is imperative to take risks and manage them. School leaders must be knowledgeable about the technologies and employment forces out there.

What is happening today is that students are participating as content producers in the world but then they come to school and are asked to maintain silence. Schools need to give them appropriate tools, guidance and resources instead.

How relevant is it to still their voices?

Education of Emotions

It is world events that shape generations and we still do not know for certain what exactly will be the long-term fallout of Covid-19 on school children who were suddenly confined to their homes. We may not know for many years the related data and analysis. But collectively, this startling change in the way they lived counts for a large-scale human trauma. These formative experiences are certain to shape their views of the world. This generation will evolve certain characteristics that we do not yet know.

Under the circumstances, what can parents and teachers do to help them prepare for the uncertainty ahead? What are the potential areas where research, reorientation and redesigning will be needed to ease their eventual entry into the new real world?

Take skill development. For the past few months, the options that have been exercised by schools and educational institutions are bound to have long-term consequences. Gen Z's (born between 1996 and 2015) training schedule has been disrupted in multiple ways. In most cases, the curriculum had to be quickly converted to online formats by amateurs in this field. Direct instructions were discarded for the most part and students and parents worked on independent projects, bolstered by digital resources. Learning struggled to happen at home amidst families and pets in spaces that call for a particular preparation. In most cases, grades were abandoned in favour of pass or fail status. Tests became a casualty and deadlines became rubber bands, stretching away merrily.

What has this loss of structure done to the children? Has it disoriented them, causing confusion and conflict? Does it mean that adults will need to exercise greater patience and be prepared to mentor and support in stronger ways? Have reorientation programs been conceived to ease their transition back to regular school when that happens? A comprehensive return would ideally involve rethinking the usual focus on academics, offering instead mentorship in making sense of their most recent experiences.

Remote learning arrangements may endure in the form of modified timetables. There have been changes in age and gender demographics. Technological improvements and the global nature of human engagement had begun to shout flexibility even before Covid-19 struck. This culture of fluidity is sure to demand new shifts and learning opportunities. Inter-generational relationships will need to be stronger than ever before; teachers will stand to benefit from being open to reverse mentoring, schools will need to devote time and resources to building a stronger multi-generational culture.

The second area that continues to create a buzz is stress management. The baseline for school students today is already higher than the generations before and research is clear that childhood exposure to sustained stress will impact mental and social development. Have schools put into place empathetic plans to assist students with their mental health struggles? The most effective stress management program is one that functions at multiple levels, home, classroom and organizational. And of these, the most sustainable results are likely to come from organizational policies.

When the classroom reopens, the young lives will resume with some form of anxiety and ambivalence. Open conversations, supportive environments, pro-active interventions will likely keep the odd minor challenge from becoming a life crisis. It will be important to remind oneself constantly of the large-scale interruption the young have experienced in all that motivated and fulfilled them earlier. The stakeholders involved will also need greater stocks of emotional intelligence than pre-pandemic. And we can no longer afford to await this skill some more years down the road ahead. The future we are looking at now will not have as much use for hard training as it will for an emotional equipment. Tomorrow's workforce, the educators, professionals and innovators will need psychological robustness and wholesomeness most of all.

What is the current rate of psychopathology of Indian teens? Do we know? Teens for instance, in the United States exhibit stress edging past that of adults. One meta-analysis (https://www.sciencedirect.com/science/article/abs/pii/S027273580900141X) says that their rate of psychopathology is five times that of 75 years ago. Lowered school achievement, unwanted pregnancy, binge drinking, use of marijuana, school violence, obesity, foggy misery, STDs…there is an overwhelming anxiety and at times acute depression during the school years. Could these be symptomatic of a complete lack of investment in the training of children's "non-cognitive" skills? Do our young have the motivation, the ability to persevere and the degree of self-control that is needed to take the economy and well-being of the race forward?

Feelings matter at home and at work. Emotion science, positive psychology and mindfulness curricula have begun to address the management of feelings. It is also called the art of managing one's micro-expressions, the frown and the smile! The ability to analyze and selectively choose emotions is related to happier outcomes in children as early as pre-school. The real benefits include deeper friendships, stronger attachments with teachers and parents, smarter conflict management, sharper academic scores and non-threatening leadership skills.

There is growing evidence by now to establish that SEL programs are effective and sorely needed in schools. The policies and funds needed however are crushingly slow in coming. How then do we begin to fund the teachers' SEL training? There are agencies that offer evidence-based SEL programming that should make support for the education of emotions easier. Nothing less than an emotional revolution is the need of the hour today. We are already a quarter way into the new century.

Has there been any dialogue in schools with the students? Do we know how they feel in the school, how different is it from what they would like to feel and what can be done to bridge the gap? It ought to be done anonymously if needed but there is a pressing case to get them to share ideas with business leaders, educators, policymakers so that the learning environments can be upgraded with a sense of urgency.

Social and emotional skills are not 'soft' but the 'hardest' we will need beginning now. A compassionate vigilance, keener empathy and a resilient adaptability will be the features of the next generation of leaders. This generation has been tested young and deserves all the support to herald the evolution of the human race they look destined to lead, God help them.

Developing a Healthy Body Image

There are terms of endearment used in several families that have the potential to damage. It is fairly common to be called *"motu"*, *"lambu"*, *"kalu"*, *"patlu"*, *"ganju"*, etc. The problem arises when the persons being addressed are not at peace with the way they look or feel and take their given name to heart. Such names may then affect their self-worth and self-confidence leading to a persistent preoccupation with appearance that is detrimental to their overall health and happiness.

Adolescents are particularly vulnerable to such inputs at a stage when they are in the process of creating their own identities with reference to the world around them. Their family environment, social media, cultural messages all influence how they regard their bodies. And the new generation of teens and young adults are extremely sensitive to thoughtless and presumptive communication.

There have been known cases of costly consequences.

Imagine a 15-year-old trolled and body-shamed for her small breasts. Are you from 'Man-chester' the bullies apparently asked her? What followed was months of depression and bouts of hysterical rage. She pulled away from her Facebook, Instagram and Twitter feeds, and from people, too. Her home became her asylum. At the next turn in this script, the teen found her way to a doctor's office to discuss surgery. She is a C-cup now; her selfies are all wow; and she got her pound of silicon!

"My friends teased me; pinched me. My self-esteem was shattered. My parents asked me to join a gym or play some sport. But how the hell am I going to run on the treadmill with the wobbly bits?" he said to a magazine. Apparently, he saw a video on YouTube for chest-reduction and found his way to a cosmetic surgeon, who suggested liposuction, and his parents played along. He is an outdoorsy person again.

These stories are not uncommon any more. It is a source of stress today to have a body that is different from the "ideal" portrayed in the media. Add to that the new epidemic of perfectionism and the peer pressure to 'fit-in' and you have double trouble. Adolescents with poor body image may suffer mood disorders and other mental health issues such as depression or anxiety, and in extreme cases, eating disorders or even body dysmorphic disorder.

There is a growing trend where Indian teenagers and pubescent youngsters – bullied, body-shamed, or simply unsatisfied with their inherited looks – are putting their noses, lips, chins, eyes, breasts and bellies under the surgeon's knife almost as a coming-of-age ceremony. And their sense of beauty is synthetic, unreal, plastic – dictated and designed by Bollywood, Hollywood, rom coms, reality television, social media. Aishwarya Rai's nose or Angelina Jolie's lips or the bootylicious figures of Beyonce and Kim Kardashian, David Beckham's calves.

There is no definitive data on the number of Indian teenagers going for cosmetic surgery, but demand seems to have grown exponentially. "The world of the Kardashians has made cosmetic surgery accessible and reduced the fear associated with it. Some 50 per cent of my patients are kids," admits Dr. Kiran Lohia of New Delhi. Doctors say that under-25s now make up nearly 70 per cent of the crowds in the OutPatient Department (OPD) clinics of cosmetic surgeons across India. "Youngsters in this age group are usually coming in before entering a new phase in their life such as starting college, a new job, or getting married," says Dr. Sunil

Choudhary, director, Institute of Aesthetic and Reconstructive Surgery, Max Healthcare, Delhi.

As parents, what are the signs that your child may be suffering from poor body image? For one, she may always be looking at her "imperfections" in the mirror. Does he avoid social situations? Are there crash diets and calorie counts being bandied about in the house? Is there negative talk about their own bodies and a need for constant reassurances? At times, the parents themselves may be overly preoccupied with appearances and food, thus setting up their children for an excess of sorts.

One wonders, where does it stop though? Teens want to look like their favourite Snapchat filters now. Dr. Neelam Vashi, founder and director of the Boston University Centre for Ethnic Skin coined the term "Snapchat dysmorphia" to explain the worrying new trend. In her recently published paper in the Journal of the American Medical Association's Facial Plastic Surgery, she says teens are increasingly altering people's perception of beauty worldwide. "A little adjusting on Facetune can smoothen out skin, make teeth look whiter and eyes and lips bigger. These filters have become the norm." And it's beginning to lead to real issues. Body dysmorphia, for example, is a condition that involves "excessive preoccupation with a perceived flaw in appearance, classified on the obsessive-compulsive spectrum."

The respectful thing to do is to help the young develop a positive body image. The adults around them can avoid comparison with other children merely on the basis of their looks. It is best to reject name calling with siblings and cousins. What can build a young spirit is to be appreciated for normative qualities such as kindness, thoughtfulness, fairness, etc. It would give them a positive push towards a future of fulfilment to be praised for their inherent and unique talents. The time, in fact, has come to communicate with the extended family to stop commenting on body image. All that is needed is a regular routine of healthy eating, physical activity and the confidence that the parents are available to discuss any concerns about their changing body image.

The young often have an inflated sense of benefit and a minimized sense of the risks involved in cosmetic surgery. Is the procedure necessary at this age, are the expectations realistic, and are the teenager and his/her parents aware of the risks involved? A detailed informed consent, effective counselling, and a cooling period to rethink the procedure are recommended. At times correctional surgery has vastly improved the quality of life of teenagers. The surgeon's scalpel has helped alleviate the nagging backache that girls with abnormally large breasts experience, or those children born with cleft lips. But others go under the knife, again and again, to cope with some inner sense of being imperfect.

The problem is that the results are not always desirable; who hasn't heard about Michael Jackson's nose falling off? "From a psychological point of view, adults seek to stand out in a crowd; teenagers want to fit in among their peers," explains psychiatrist Dr. Ambrish Dharmadhikari of Mumbai.

The prudent thing is to keep an open mind, connect and communicate with honesty and compassion. The stakes here are higher than they have ever been.

Combating Drugs

Our kids are bored today like never before. And there are these demons dancing in their little minds. It is almost as though they have lost their sense of wonderment. We are too busy to look at them with light and love; we just want to get on with the business of them succeeding. In the absence of that all important affirmative vibe at home and at school, very often, they feel the need to 'feel' something, to try something new.

Concerns were raised in the Rajya Sabha recently over children falling into the trap of drugs, with a Congress member claiming that 25,000 school children in Delhi have turned addicts. In Punjab, an alarming 75 per cent of its youth is said to be severely habituated. Mumbai, Hyderabad and other cities around the country are quickly getting on to this train of grief. Distressingly so, the age of initiation gets younger and younger. A research published by the Indian Journal of

Psychiatry reveals that in India, by the time most children reach the ninth grade, about 50 per cent have tried at least one of the illicit drugs.

However, this is not a time to be alarmed. Our young are as dismayed and confused when these substances appear in their young lives. What we can do is to listen to them from a position of knowledge.

So to begin with, let's acknowledge that the taboo around drug use and abuse is losing ground fast. It was once considered the preserve of "naughty children" but that distinction is long gone.

Vaping and Juuling are the new gateways for coping and self-soothing. These are covert methods for ingesting nicotine and marijuana (pot/cannabis/weed/ganja/charas/bhang). Addiction can happen in a matter of weeks and young people are fascinated with the paraphernalia around it — the tanks, the mods, the Juul, the chargers and the pods. Most of these devices fit neatly up one's sleeves or in a pocket of jeans or a backpack and because the output is vapor, it is either odorless or has a child friendly smell like that of bubble gum or cereal.

Aside from vaping, Juuling and marijuana, the abuse of prescription drugs in India is gaining momentum. According to the United Nations Office on Drugs & Crime (UNODC) even though the law requires all drugs with "abuse potential" to be sold only on prescription, there is "significant diversion" from this. Sale of these lethal cocktails ranging from uppers to downers, benzodiazepines to hallucinogens is reflected in increased emergency room visits, overdose deaths and treatment admissions for prescription drug use disorder. Teens themselves are also rather casual about dealing drugs. They will buy and sell for a select group of friends. And girls are now nearly as likely as boys to use regularly.

Today when a child mentions paper, do not jump to the conclusion that he is referring to chart paper! More and more young people take to weed, rolling joints that many parents and teachers cannot tell from regular cigarettes. There is an enticing cultural vibe around this substance moreover and plenty of fallacies of convenience. Children believe it is a plant, from the earth, far safer than alcohol because it does not tax a vital organ. The notion is that while weed smokers are recreational, it is the alcohol drinkers that are hardcore.

But weed today is a deceptively dangerous substance. For one, it is the most de-motivating drug out there associated with erasure of memories and loss of life's essential spark. If the child is all of a sudden markedly lazy, elusive, the grades drop, he loses interest in the activities he once loved, if he changes friends, or if he starts to have trouble at school, parents and teachers are to trust their instinct and ask the question. The tipping point happens when smoking weed shifts from being recreational to being medicinal. Young people begin to smoke not just to get high or stoned but to soothe anxiety, manage depression, numb feelings about falling grades or family or social issues. A lot of kids smoke at night to fall asleep. With no peace of mind, they try to medicate consciousness away, it is an effective escape from one's own psyche. The risk is in losing time and potential and connection with others. No longer just through bowls, joints and bongs, weed can be vaped, Juuled, baked into brownies or edibles, distilled into wax like dabs and lollipops too.

Worryingly so, weed is a different drug altogether today, wildly more potent and addictive than before. Some of the most commonly used strains are as much as 20 or 30 times higher in THC (tetrahydrocannabinol, the mind altering substance in weed) than the drug was 30 years ago. Weed is unregulated since it is illegal still and it may come laced with some other drug like heroin, meth (methamphetamine), LSD (lysergic acid diethylamide/acid) or PCP (phencyclidine/ angel dust). Weed is also notoriously easy to acquire today. Ask any square and scrubbed teenager and they will know dealer names, cell numbers and houses. Its distribution channels are clean; you don't need to go heading into the dingy parts of cities, just regular spaces.

If your child is abusing drug of any kind, the thing to do would be to first listen fully and completely without agenda and fear and judgment. Instead of focusing on the behaviour that seems unacceptable to us therefore, focus on the why. Why do they use substance so frequently? What feelings does the drug protect them from? How else might they cope? Better be sincere and kind and have unconditional positive regard. Our children have ultra-sensitive detectors that ping at patronizing and vilifying and bullshitting. Kids are known to keep their consumption moderate when they can talk to their parents about it. A 'don't ask don't tell' policy would be as foolhardy a cat-and-mouse game as the "search and destroy" theory in these circumstances. It might in fact be time to reach out to a therapist or addictions specialist for help.

Weed is nearing legalization and that will increase its usage and bolster the thinking that there is no downside, this is not true. Future red flags would look like a semester lost, friendships strained, and family relationships in turmoil.

Social inclusion, emotional resilience and normative training would be the way to go. To resolve this humanitarian crisis it might help to constantly remind ourselves that the opposite of addiction is connection.

The Cinderella Syndrome

This psychological condition has become particularly relevant today, as it has evolved in this era of modern societal pressures, unrealistic expectations, and the pervasive influence of media and social platforms. Cinderella was rescued from her forsaken circumstances into remarkable fortune by her "fairy godmother" and "prince". And much like her, today our young generation harbours unrealistic expectations that life will improve dramatically through an external force. They wait for outside validation to rescue them from their current situation, expecting that once this happens, their lives will magically transform, like Cinderella's in the fairy tale.

But isn't this syndrome deeply rooted in our childhood stories of Sleeping Beauty and Snow White too? They all perpetuate the idea that happiness, success, and fulfilment come not through hard work and personal development but through the intervention of an external force – often a romantic partner, wealth, or fame. While these stories were once harmless bedtime tales, the messages they convey are affecting the worldview of our young. The internalized ideals begin to slowly translate into real world expectations leading many to subconsciously wait for their lives to change without taking proactive steps to shape their own futures. With the rise of social media and celebrity culture, these narratives have taken on a new dimension, making the Cinderella Syndrome more prevalent and damaging.

How does the Cinderella Syndrome manifest?

Take career expectations and the quick-fix mentality. With the rise of the "hustle culture" and the glorification of startup success stories, many young people believe that overnight success is not only possible but the standard. They idolize tech moguls like Elon Musk and Mark Zuckerberg, who seem to have achieved fame and fortune with ease. This can lead to unrealistic career expectations. Instead of focusing on long-term growth, skill development, and gradual progress, young people might expect immediate results and feel disillusioned when success doesn't come quickly. This quick-fix mentality can also manifest in the pursuit of "side hustles" and "get-rich-quick" schemes, further perpetuating the belief that one grand opportunity will change their lives forever.

Take their all-too-common wait for a "perfect" relationship. With the rise of dating apps and curated social media posts, many young people are bombarded with the idea that there is a "perfect" partner who will sweep them off their feet and solve all their problems. This belief can lead to several negative outcomes. Some may remain in unfulfilling or toxic relationships, hoping that their partner will eventually change and become the prince or princess they've always dreamed of. Others might hop from one relationship to the next, constantly searching for someone who meets their unrealistic expectations, leading to a cycle of disappointment and dissatisfaction.

Take social media's portrayal of the "perfect" life. Social media has amplified the Cinderella Syndrome by allowing users to present curated, idealized versions of their lives. Influencers and celebrities frequently post about their luxurious vacations, perfect relationships, and glamorous lifestyles, leading many young people to believe that a similar life is within reach if they find the right partner, the right job, or the right look. This constant exposure to seemingly perfect lives can exacerbate feelings of inadequacy, causing individuals to become passive in their own lives, waiting for a dramatic transformation or a sudden stroke of luck to bring them happiness and success. There is an illusion of effortless transformation.

Take family and cultural pressures. The pressure to succeed, marry, and achieve specific milestones is intense. This can contribute to the Cinderella Syndrome by reinforcing the belief that success or happiness comes from fulfilling societal expectations, rather than from personal growth or self-discovery. In societies where marriage, for example, is seen as a necessary step toward adulthood or happiness, young people may feel even more inclined to wait for the "right" partner to rescue them from societal judgment or family pressure.

There are some real dangers of the Cinderella Syndrome. It can lead to several detrimental outcomes, both psychologically and socially. For individuals, the constant waiting for an external force to bring happiness can result in stagnation, anxiety, and depression. As they passively wait for life to change, they may neglect opportunities for personal growth and development, leading to frustration when their dreams remain unfulfilled. From a societal perspective, the Cinderella Syndrome perpetuates harmful gender norms and ideals. It reinforces the notion that women, in particular, need to be rescued or validated by a man, rather than encouraging them to be self-sufficient and empowered. This not only limits individual potential but also contributes to broader systemic inequalities.

How then does one overcome the Cinderella Syndrome? It is crucial for individuals, families, and society at large to shift the narrative around success, happiness, and fulfilment. The first thing to do is to promote personal agency. Instead of waiting for external forces to change their lives, young people should be encouraged to take ownership of their futures. This means setting realistic goals, taking small but meaningful steps toward those goals, and understanding that success often comes from consistent effort rather than from magical transformations.

Media representations moreover need to be challenged. Media literacy is more important than ever in the age of social media. Young people need to be taught to critically evaluate the content they consume, particularly the idealized versions of life presented by influencers and celebrities. Understanding that much of what they see online is curated and filtered can help reduce feelings of inadequacy and the pressure to live up to unrealistic standards. Parents, educators, and influencers themselves can contribute to this shift by promoting authentic, honest representations of life and success, rather than perpetuating the fantasy of effortless transformation.

This is the time to foster emotional independence. While romantic partnerships can bring joy and fulfilment, they should not be seen as the sole source of happiness. Young people should be taught to cultivate their own sense of self-worth and fulfilment outside of their relationships, so they don't fall into the trap of waiting for someone else to "complete" them.

Society's definition of success needs to evolve. Rather than focusing solely on external markers like wealth, status, or relationships, success should be defined in terms of personal growth, fulfilment, and meaningful contributions to society.

The Cinderella Syndrome is a pervasive psychological phenomenon that has significant implications for the young generation today.

We can help young people break free from the fairy tale mindset and create their own paths to fulfilment. Our narratives around success and happiness need to reflect a more balanced, realistic, and empowering vision for the future.

Perfect shoes are not enough to change one's life. It takes walking in those shoes!

Balancing Compassion and Consequences

What is that one value all humans everywhere strive to strike? A balance. It is a universally accepted attribute of a wholesome life.

However, the cultural headwinds today are weakening adult leadership that can help the young achieve a healthy balance in their lives. Bosses, teachers, coaches, and parents tread on egg shells around children today because the popular script is that "our young are under too much pressure and we cannot afford to stress them out further." We are all in the midst of a massive cultural push to extend compassion and empathy to our over-stimulated young.

Adults often fear drawing boundaries with their children and wards due to a variety of emotional, psychological, and societal factors. One of the primary reasons is the fear of damaging the parent-child relationship. Many parents worry that setting firm boundaries might lead to conflict, resentment, or a breakdown in communication. This fear is often compounded by guilt, especially if the parents feel they are not spending enough time with their children due to work or other obligations. They may compensate by being overly lenient, hoping to maintain their child's affection and avoid feelings of inadequacy.

Another reason adults hesitate to set boundaries is the desire to be seen as a "cool" or "understanding" parent. In a world where social media and peer pressure influence parenting styles, there is a temptation to be more of a friend than a parent. This approach may stem from the fear of being labelled as strict or old-fashioned, leading to a reluctance to enforce rules and expectations.

In that process, we have lost sight of the interplay between compassion and consequences. This is a theme that will resonate deeply with every adult who is remotely concerned with the growth of young people. The fact is that for the truest success in life, our next generation will need to experience both.

Let me share a story from my teenage years that captures this balance. Growing up in India, I was witness to my brother being surrounded by friends, who, like him, were brimming with youthful energy and reckless ideas. I vividly remember the day he turned 17 and got his chocolate-coloured Hero Majestic Moped. I was as ecstatic as his friends to hit the road on this new steed with him.

One afternoon, a friend had the idea that we should try something daring. My brother would drive the moped with me as his pillion, and another would ride on a bicycle, holding on to the moped. It seemed thrilling, the kind of excitement only a teenager would crave.

So, there we were, his friend touched the moped with one toe, balancing on the bike with the other, as we accelerated down the road.

Everything seemed fun until, out of nowhere, we were caught by my friend's father, who happened to be driving behind us. He saw everything, and unlike what we expected, didn't immediately scold us. Instead, he chuckled, probably remembering his own youthful days, and let us off with a warning. But the story didn't end there.

Our father, on the other hand, wasn't amused when he heard what happened. When we got home, he sat us down and asked, "Did you think about what could have gone wrong?" At that moment, I realized I hadn't. The fun had blinded me to the potential dangers. Our father didn't shout or lecture us endlessly. Instead, he calmly explained the risks and then handed down a consequence: my brother was grounded for two weeks, his driving privileges revoked.

It was a tough lesson, but it was fair. Our father's approach combined compassion with consequences, ensuring that we understood the gravity of our actions without feeling crushed by guilt. This balance taught us both to think before acting, a lesson that has stayed with us I would like to believe.

In India, where the value of respect for elders and authority is deeply ingrained, the lessons of compassion and consequences often go hand-in-hand. I recall another story that made headlines not long ago, involving a young student who was caught cheating during an exam. His mother, instead of covering up for him or pleading with the authorities, made him own up to his mistake. She walked him to the principal's office and insisted that he face the consequences of his actions. The boy was suspended for a week, but during that time, his mother didn't just punish him. She sat with him, helped him understand the importance of integrity, and worked through his studies together.

These stories, though different in context, highlight the same principle. Compassion doesn't mean letting someone off the hook; it means caring enough to ensure they understand the consequences of their actions. This is a lesson that echoes through the generations in India, where parents, teachers, and community leaders often walk the fine line between nurturing and disciplining.

Compassion without consequences can lead to a sense of entitlement, where young people might begin to believe that they can evade accountability. On the other hand, consequences without compassion can breed resentment. The real challenge lies in blending the two, creating an environment where young people feel supported even as they learn from their mistakes. Children, who grow up without clear boundaries, may struggle with self-discipline, respect for authority, and understanding the concept of limits. The lack of structure, moreover, can lead to difficulties in school, social relationships, and later in professional environments where rules and boundaries are essential for success.

Time and again, it has been seen that young people raised without boundaries often lack the ability to cope with frustration and disappointment. Without the experience of being told "no" or being held accountable for their actions, they may have unrealistic expectations of life and struggle with resilience. This can result in emotional instability, poor decision-making, and an inability to handle the challenges of adulthood. In the long term, the absence of boundaries can lead to a lack of respect for others' rights and feelings. Without the early lessons that boundaries provide, individuals may become self-centred, disregarding the needs and limits of others in their personal and professional lives. This can lead to strained relationships, both personally and professionally, and hinder their ability to function effectively in society.

Ultimately, while setting boundaries may be challenging for adults, it is a crucial aspect of responsible parenting. Clear boundaries provide children with a sense of security, structure, and understanding of the world around them. They learn the importance of rules, respect, and self-control, which are essential for their development into well-adjusted, responsible, and empathetic adults.

In the end, it's about preparing them for the realities of life. Whether it's the judge who refused to lower the sentence for a hungry young man who resorted to theft or the mother who turned in her son after recognizing him in a security photo, the message is clear: true compassion involves guiding someone towards better choices, not shielding them from the repercussions of their actions.

So, as we navigate our roles as mentors, parents, and leaders, let's remember this balance. By standing firm in our principles while offering a hand to those who stumble, we can help shape a future generation that is both compassionate and responsible.

The Harm That AI Can Cause

In a shocking incident (https://tinyurl.com/aimisuse) at a reputed CBSE school in Bengaluru, a parent of a class 9 student has filed a police complaint regarding the spread of AI-generated inappropriate photos of her daughter on social media. This disturbing event has quite understandably rattled the school community, raising serious concerns about privacy, cyberbullying, and the misuse of technology among students. Another student from the same class also had their images manipulated, though no formal complaint has been filed in that case.

The issue surfaced when the AI-generated images were shared in a private Instagram group chat with around 20 classmates of the victim. Although the affected student was not part of the group, her friends informed her about it. She was deeply disturbed by this violation and suspects that the images were taken from her private Instagram account. This leads her to believe that someone she knows, possibly a friend, could be responsible for this harmful act. This is what one would call a jugular betrayal!

Unfortunately, this is not an isolated incident. It is part of a growing global trend where technology is misused to harm individuals, especially minors. In recent years, there have been numerous cases worldwide involving AI-generated and altered images used to harass and intimidate young people.

In the United States, a significant case occurred in 2020 (https://tinyurl.com/aimischief) when a mother in Pennsylvania was charged with creating deepfake videos of her daughter's cheerleading rivals. The AI-generated videos showed the girls in compromising positions, causing severe emotional distress to the victims.

In October 2023, some 10th grade girls at Westfield High School, New Jersey alerted administrators that boys in their class had used artificial intelligence software to fabricate sexually explicit images of them and were circulating the faked pictures (https://tinyurl.com/epidemicteenfakes).

It is a wakeup call for those responsible for the health of our youth. Nearly 21% of the Indian population is adolescent (about 243 million). They make a formidable demographic and economic force. And their mental and emotional wellbeing is the nation's collective responsibility. Given the challenge of meeting their varied needs, life circumstances, and socio-economic conditions, artificially induced mischief is unaffordable.

All these unfortunate incidents emphasize the urgent need for schools to take proactive measures to protect their students from such digital threats. It is impossible to predict what long-term harm could befall these hapless young victims given the persistent nature of online content. What key steps could a school therefore take to check this harmful trend?

The time has come for schools to implement comprehensive digital literacy programs that teach students about responsible technology use, the importance of privacy, and the dangers of sharing personal information online. These programs should also cover the ethical implications of AI and other emerging technologies. Both the perpetrators and the victims deserve to know the nature of this beast known as the unchecked and uncivilized technology.

No such measures will be effective, however, unless and until schools begin to put in place some strong cybersecurity policies. This would include guidelines on the acceptable use of school networks and devices, as well as clear protocols for reporting and addressing cyberbullying and online harassment.

Another potent defence would be to hold regular workshops for students, teachers, and parents on topics like cyber safety, digital footprints, and the risks of social media. This way, schools will build a well-informed community.

Schools will have to prepare themselves to provide counselling and support services for students affected by cyberbullying and digital harassment. These experiences can be devastating, bringing intense shame upon those affected, leaving them to face a lifetime of struggle with their sense of self-worth and identity. Trained counsellors can make a life and death difference at this point by helping victims cope with the psychological impact.

Teachers would do well to stay vigilant and aware of the signs of cyberbullying and digital harassment. They should encourage students to report any suspicious or harmful online activities and ensure that such reports are taken seriously and addressed promptly. It is crucial to foster a classroom environment where students feel safe and supported. Teachers will have to get into the rhythm of promoting inclusivity, respect, and empathy among students and actively discourage any form of bullying or harassment.

Would an evolution of the school curriculum to include discussions on digital ethics, privacy, and the responsible use of technology help students understand the impact of their online actions? Absolutely, and more so when teachers begin to use real-world examples and case studies to illustrate these concepts effectively. Just as important, is for the teachers to engineer an effective communication and collaboration with parents and guardians. Never has the oft quoted dictum of "It takes a village to raise a child" been more true. It has become crucial for teachers to regularly update parents on the school's policies and initiatives related to digital safety and encourage them to discuss these topics with their children at home.

And technology can help here. It can monitor students' online activities within the school's network to help identify potential issues early on. The tricky part in this exercise, however, would be to maintain respect for students' privacy and act in accordance with legal and ethical guidelines.

The Bengaluru school incident involving AI-generated inappropriate photos is a stark reminder of the challenges posed by advanced technology in the hands of malicious individuals. It highlights the urgent need for comprehensive measures to protect students from digital threats. Schools are being called upon to stay a step ahead by taking proactive steps to educate their communities, implement robust policies, and provide the necessary support to victims. Teachers, as frontline defenders of student wellbeing, play a pivotal role in these efforts. By working together, schools, teachers, parents, and students can create a safer and more respectful digital environment for all.

There is no way to sugarcoat this. We are in a horrific new era of ultrarealistic, AI-generated, child sexual abuse images. The offenders are using downloadable open-source generative AI models, which can produce images to crushing effects. What is even more alarming is the speed of the development and the potential for irreversible mischief it creates.

The Three Cs of Modern Education

We are in an era that is defined by rapid technological advancement, globalization, and societal shifts. These phenomena are throwing formidable challenges at the traditional model of education. The evolving demands of the workforce demand more than just textbook knowledge from the employees. It has therefore become essential for educators to cultivate three indispensable skills in the young – critical thinking, creativity, and collaboration, so that they may thrive in an increasingly complex world.

How may these skills be nurtured in educational settings? What strategies would prepare students for the challenges of the future?

Critical thinking is the ability to analyze information objectively, evaluate its credibility, and make informed decisions. In today's information-rich society, where misinformation spreads rapidly, it is more vital than ever. Students who develop critical thinking skills become adept at questioning assumptions, examining evidence, and reasoning logically.

Imagine a high school classroom discussing a controversial social issue like climate change. Instead of passively accepting information presented by the teacher or media, students engage in critical discussions, evaluating different perspectives, scrutinizing data, and forming their own opinions based on evidence. This not only enhances their understanding of the topic but also cultivates their ability to think independently.

Critical thinking is the cornerstone of effective decision-making, problem-solving, and analytical reasoning. It is the only way for students to make sense of the information-saturated landscape they are surrounded by today. And educators play a pivotal role in fostering a culture of critical inquiry within classrooms.

One approach is to integrate inquiry-based learning methodologies that encourage students to ask questions, challenge assumptions, and explore multiple perspectives. By engaging in debates, discussions, and projects that require evidence-based reasoning, students develop the ability to think critically and make informed judgments.

Moreover, teaching critical thinking involves nurturing metacognitive skills – awareness of one's own thought processes. Through reflection and self-assessment, students learn to identify biases, assess the reliability of sources, and revise their thinking based on new information. By embedding critical thinking across the curriculum, educators empower students to navigate complexities and adapt to diverse challenges.

Creativity is the second crucial C of modern education. It is the ability to think divergently, generate original ideas, and solve problems innovatively. In today's rapidly changing world, where automation is reshaping industries and creating new challenges, creativity has emerged as a prized asset. Students who harness their creative potential are better equipped to adapt to change, think outside the box, and innovate solutions to complex problems.

Imagine a middle school art class where students are tasked with creating a piece of multimedia artwork inspired by a current social issue. Through this project, students not only explore their artistic abilities but also learn to express their ideas creatively, communicate messages effectively, and address real-world issues through innovative means. This nurtures their creative thinking skills and prepares them to become adaptable problem solvers in any field.

Creativity is the catalyst for innovation, entrepreneurship, and adaptability in an ever-changing world. Yet, traditional educational models often prioritize rote memorization over creative expression. To unlock students' creative potential, educators must create environments that nurture curiosity, experimentation, and divergent thinking.

One strategy is to incorporate project-based learning experiences that encourage students to solve real-world problems through creative solutions. Whether designing inventions, composing music, or crafting visual artworks, students learn to think imaginatively and embrace ambiguity.

Educators can further leverage technology as a tool for creative expression. From digital media production to coding and design, technology offers numerous avenues for students to unleash their creativity and collaborate on interdisciplinary projects. It is by celebrating diversity of thought and encouraging risk-taking that educators cultivate a culture where creativity thrives, empowering students to become innovators and change-makers.

The third crucial C of modern education is collaboration. It is the ability to work effectively with others, communicate ideas, and leverage diverse perspectives to achieve common goals. In today's interconnected world, where globalization and technology facilitate collaboration across geographical boundaries, the ability to collaborate is paramount. Students who excel in collaboration develop strong interpersonal skills, empathy, and an appreciation for teamwork.

Picture a group of high-school students participating in a project-based learning activity where they are tasked with designing and building a sustainable community garden for their school. In this collaborative endeavour, students assume different roles, delegate tasks, and coordinate efforts to bring their vision to life. Through this experience, they not only learn to communicate effectively but also develop essential teamwork skills such as leadership, compromise, and conflict resolution.

Collaboration has emerged as a vital skill for success in a hyperconnected world. Whether in the workplace or within communities, the ability to collaborate effectively is essential for tackling complex challenges and driving collective progress. And educators can foster collaboration by incorporating cooperative learning structures that promote teamwork, communication, and conflict resolution skills. Through group projects, peer-to-peer feedback, and collaborative problem-solving tasks, students learn to leverage their collective strengths and perspectives.

In addition, global collaboration initiatives provide students with opportunities to connect with peers from diverse backgrounds, fostering cross-cultural understanding and empathy. Virtual exchange programs, joint research projects, and international partnerships broaden students' horizons and prepare them for global citizenship. By emphasizing the value of collaboration and nurturing interpersonal skills, educators equip students with the tools to navigate diverse social dynamics and work collaboratively towards common goals.

The three Cs of modern education – critical thinking, creativity, and collaboration – are indispensable skills that empower students to thrive in the complex and interconnected world of the 21st century. By fostering these skills, educators can prepare students not only for academic success but also for lifelong learning and meaningful engagement in society. As we continue to adapt to the challenges and opportunities of the digital age, prioritizing the development of these skills becomes imperative in shaping a future generation equipped to tackle the unknown with confidence and resilience.

In a world we live today, the role of education extends beyond imparting knowledge to cultivating essential skills for lifelong success. Through inquiry-based learning, project-based experiences, and collaborative initiatives, educators can create dynamic learning environments where students develop the skills and mindset needed to navigate ambiguity, innovate boldly, and collaborate effectively. As we look towards the future, the smart thing to do is to envision an educational landscape where every student is empowered to think critically, create passionately, and collaborate purposefully – where education becomes not only a preparation for life but a lifelong journey of growth and discovery.

The Peer Pressure of Tomorrow

In 2023, 26 suicides, and 5 in first 2 months of 2024, along with 3 disappearances. These tragic events shook Kota, Rajasthan, a coaching hub for the JEE and NEET exams. Stress, depression, and despair are rampant there due to tough competition and unavoidable peer pressure.

Peer pressure has always been a powerful force, especially during adolescence. With the rise of social media, however, it's taken on a new form. It is true that social media connects people and shares information, but it also intensifies peer pressure. The constant comparisons create unrealistic standards, making many individuals feel inadequate.

Recognizing the impact of social media-induced peer pressure is crucial. But how does one tackle it? Schools need to promote digital literacy, encourage open communication, foster self-reflection, set realistic expectations, and build offline connections. This way, students can navigate the digital world with resilience and authenticity, balancing both the positive and negative aspects of social media.

Looking ahead to 2035, one wonders how peer pressure will evolve! Can young people be readied for this emerging landscape? To thrive in a digital world while maintaining authenticity and mental wellbeing, they'll clearly need new skills, knowledge, and support systems.

Though predicting the exact evolution of peer pressure is challenging, we can certainly speculate based on ongoing trends and emerging technologies. One certainty is that peer pressure will intertwine more with digital platforms, like virtual reality, augmented reality, and immersive online experiences. Artificial Intelligence (AI) algorithms are already shaping user behaviour, and personalized content tailored to individual preferences could likely create echo chambers, reinforcing existing viewpoints and potentially isolating individuals from diverse perspectives. Then there is the phenomenon of biometric data and wearable technology for instance, where individuals might feel pressured to maintain certain health metrics or lifestyle choices.

More and more it seems, that we must start early for a healthier future. Comprehensive digital literacy education should be integrated into school curricula, equipping students with critical thinking skills to navigate emerging technologies and distinguish between authentic and manipulated information. As the world becomes more interconnected, peer pressure may transcend geographical boundaries. Imagine all the globalized communication facilitated by social media impacting and threatening local cultures and social dynamics. This is where emotional intelligence becomes a crucial skill. Teaching our young to manage emotions, build empathy, and make informed decisions would enhance resilience against negative peer influences, both online and offline.

We are already seeing a shift towards more niche and specialized online communities, intensifying conformity within those niches. Fostering critical thinking skills is sure to empower individuals to question information, challenge social norms constructively, and make decisions aligned with their values. Creating a culture of independent thought and respectful disagreement is essential.

Mental health awareness has been growing. Future dynamics may shift towards promoting wellbeing, with peer support, acceptance of vulnerability, and destigmatization of seeking help becoming integral components of social dynamics. This points in the direction of integrating mental health education into school curricula, providing coping mechanisms and support systems to address mental health challenges associated with peer pressure and online interactions. Leveraging technology for mental health support could become a life and death issue, with accessible resources, counselling services, and peer support networks.

It is evident around us that positive peer pressure is evolving towards collaborative efforts for social impact. Many of our young feel compelled to participate in collective actions, environmental initiatives, or community projects, tying social validation to contributions to the greater good. This is a long due and welcome shift. Promoting positive online communities that celebrate diversity, inclusivity, and authenticity is therefore vital. Teaching students to find and contribute to supportive digital environments aligned with their interests and values has become essential.

Take the case of dynamic cultural norms and societal expectations. Our future generations will witness shifts in what is considered socially acceptable. Parental and caregiver involvement will become a key factor here. They will be called upon to equip themselves with tools to understand the digital landscape, engage in open conversations with their children, and provide guidance on setting boundaries.

There is nothing like an emphasis on education about digital wellbeing and mental health to equip future generations to navigate peer pressure healthily. Only critical thinking skills and emotional intelligence can help shape positive social dynamics. This would involve guidance on healthy online behaviours, responsible social media use, understanding the impact of cyberbullying, and fostering positive digital relationships crucial. Encouraging open communication between parents, educators, and young individuals about their online experiences is essential.

Advocating for the ethical design of technology platforms is additionally vital. App developers and designers have to be urged to prioritize user wellbeing, implementing features promoting positive interactions, and minimizing harmful algorithms.

Establishing a continuous feedback loop amongst researchers, educators, and technology developers will keep all the stakeholders informed about emerging trends, potential risks, and effective strategies. Regularly updating educational programs and support systems is necessary to address the evolving nature of peer pressure.

As we move forward, it is not merely about preparing for the challenges presented by the peer pressure of tomorrow but actively shaping a future where technology enhances our collective wellbeing, individuality is celebrated, and our shared spaces foster diverse perspectives and informed decision-making. Only through a concerted effort to balance technological progress with human values can we navigate the complex interplay between AI and peer dynamics in the decades to come.

We truly stand on the cusp of a future shaped by the integration of artificial intelligence into our social fabric. This brings us both unprecedented opportunities and challenges. We must think ahead with the objective of enabling all to shine in a digital world while staying true to oneself.

Let's create a future where everyone feels wholesome, seen, strong, and confident!

Sporting Horizons

The dynamics of sports culture have undergone major transformations in recent years. At the forefront of this brave new horizon is the new generation. The young are reshaping societal values, technology integration, and the overall engagement with sports. What are the multifaceted aspects that are driving this change? What are the perspectives of the next generation of athletes and fans? What are the key elements in the changing role of sports in a broader social context?

In the digital age, technology has completely changed the game, shaping the way fans interact with sports in significant ways. The rise of digital platforms, social media, and streaming services has revolutionized the sports landscape. Gone are the days of traditional television broadcasts. Fans have a never before flexibility and accessibility to the world of sports with online streaming.

Athletes are no longer distant figures, they have become influencers, offering fans direct access to their lives through platforms like Instagram, Twitter, and TikTok.

This shift towards digital engagement has democratized content creation, turning fans into active contributors to the sports conversation. Fans now share highlights, provide commentary, and even create their own sports-related content, blurring the lines between athletes and their audience. This participatory culture has created a shared experience that goes beyond the confines of the game. There is a new sense of community in the world of sports.

This new connectedness forms the basis for strong voices in favour of inclusivity and diversity, deemed imperatives by young sportspersons. The new generation emphasizes the need for sports to be more representative and welcoming, transcending barriers of gender, race, sexual orientation, and physical abilities. This call for inclusivity extends beyond player rosters to leadership roles, coaching staff, and decision-making positions within sports organizations.

However, challenges continue to persist, with a continuing dissatisfaction regarding the industry's embrace of diversity. The historic bias favouring heterosexual cisgender males, for instance, remains evident, prompting figures like Lewis Hamilton and Jake Daniels to advocate for change within Formula 1 and professional football. However, there are encouraging signs of progress, as demonstrated by the 2021 Tokyo Olympics, which marked a milestone as the most gender-equal in history.

Initiatives such as 'The See It Achieve It' aim to support black, Asian, and minority ethnic players in the Women's Super League, and influential figures like Megan

Rapinoe continue to champion equality, applying pressure on the sports industry to evolve.

The new generation is also reshaping the notion of competition in sports. While the traditional emphasis on winning holds strong, there is a growing appreciation for sports integrity, fair play, and the journey of self-improvement. The hyper-competitive, win-at-all-costs mentality is being challenged, with a greater emphasis on the positive aspects of sports, such as teamwork, resilience, and personal growth. This shift reflects the desire for sports to be more than just a battleground for victories; it should also be a space for fostering values that extend beyond the scoreboard. The emphasis on the journey, learning, and camaraderie is indicative of a broader societal shift towards a more holistic and positive approach to competition. Competition today is being defined as a phenomenon beyond merely winning or losing.

One of the major shifts emerging from this evolving sports culture has been athlete activism. Athletes are leveraging their platforms to address social and political issues, transcending the traditional boundaries of sports in potent ways. The willingness of athletes to be outspoken on issues they are passionate about challenges the notion that sports and politics should remain separate. From racial justice to climate change, athletes are engaging in activism that resonates with the new generation of fans. Social media plays a pivotal role in this arena of social change, providing a direct line of communication to a global audience. Sports have moved beyond the confines of entertainment to become a powerful tool for social change. Athletes and sports organizations have begun to exercise a cultural impact well beyond the scoreboard.

The most heartening shift in the changing sports culture has been evident in the way mental health has come to be addressed within the athletic community. High-profile athletes like Simone Biles and Naomi Osaka openly discussing their struggles have sparked a broader and kinder conversation about mental health in sports. Younger individuals advocate for a more empathetic and supportive approach within the sports industry, challenging the perception that vulnerability is a weakness.

This growing new recognition that athletes are human beings with emotional well-being needs is reshaping how sports organizations approach mental health support for their athletes. This is symbolic of a broader societal acknowledgment of the importance of mental well-being and a new commitment to dismantling the stigma surrounding mental health issues.

The sports culture of the new generation is undeniably, a progressive and dynamic force, shaped by technological advancements, a commitment to inclusivity and diversity, a redefined approach to competition, athlete activism, and an expanded understanding of the role of sports in society. As these dynamics continue to push the sporting horizons, the sports landscape will likely witness further transformations. A new era of sports playing a potent catalyst for positive change and social progress is upon the world.

As educators, an understanding of and acceptance of these reorientations in sporting culture can provide valuable insights into the evolving perspectives of the students they mentor. It is time to create opportunities for discussions that go beyond the game, delving into themes of inclusivity, resilience, and the broader impact sports can have on society. Contemporary students will need help to shape their sports ecosystem based on the new values and aspirations.

For India, this significant change in the global sports landscape is accompanied with a hectic transformation in its infrastructure. The combined efforts of the government, private entities, and the growing interest among the people are driving the nation towards sporting excellence on the global stage. Indian sports are on the brink of a new era, marked by rising talents, enhanced infrastructure, and a fervent embrace of diverse disciplines. A promising horizon beckons the Indian athletes.

The Metaverse in Schools

The metaverse is a concept that we once saw and read of only in science fiction. Neal Stephenson's science fiction novel *Snow Crash*, published in 1992 featured the Metaverse, a collective virtual space in a dystopian future inhabited by avatars of real people. It was a world where people could interact, conduct business, and navigate the digital realm, blurring the lines between the physical and virtual worlds. This once fictional space is rapidly becoming a tangible reality today. It is reshaping human interaction with digital environments.

With advancing technology, the metaverse holds great potential for revolutionizing education. There will be immersive and interactive experiences that are bound to transcend the limitations of traditional classrooms. The question to ask is: what would be the possibilities, challenges, and implications of integrating the metaverse into educational settings? What will the future look like when virtual worlds become dynamic extensions of the learning environment?

To begin with, what is the metaverse? It is a collective virtual shared space that combines aspects of social media, online gaming, augmented reality (AR), and virtual reality (VR) to create an immersive and interconnected digital universe. Unlike traditional online spaces, the metaverse is not confined to a single platform; instead, it spans multiple interconnected virtual worlds, each offering unique experiences and opportunities for interaction. When applied in education, the metaverse will be able to create immersive learning environments. Imagine the students stepping right into historical events, exploring scientific concepts at a molecular level, or even travelling to distant planets – all within the virtual realm. An experiential learning of this degree will foster a much deeper understanding and engagement with the subject.

The metaverse brings huge advantages to the classroom. It breaks down geographical barriers, bringing together students from different parts of the world to collaborate seamlessly. Virtual classrooms become a melting pot of cultural exchange and diverse perspectives that make the learning experience that much richer. This global collaboration at the school level prepares the students for a connected and interdependent world.

The metaverse moreover, can be as personal as it is universal. Imagine the power of tailoring educational content to individual learning styles and preferences! The metaverse brings in adaptive technologies capable of tracking student progress while adjusting the difficulty of tasks and simultaneously providing real-time feedback. Students can then be free to master core concepts at their own pace.

One of essential challenges with the traditional system of education has been to bridge the gap between theoretical knowledge and real-world application. Virtual simulations within the metaverse offers opportunities for career exploration and skill development. Students can avail of hands-on experiences in a multitude of professions, ranging from engineering to healthcare to the arts. They can explore potential careers, develop practical skills, and make informed decisions about their future paths. The metaverse can also be designed to make it accessible to students with disabilities and different learning styles.

The metaverse almost sounds too good to be true! And there are serious challenges involved in integrating it into the educational system. The primary issue is of ensuring equitable access. How do you provide every school with the necessary infrastructure, such as high-speed internet, VR/AR devices, and powerful computing resources? If left unaddressed, these disparities are certain to cause a digital divide in education. The metaverse also has as much potential for abuse as it does for use. To be able to navigate the space with responsibility, students will need to develop commensurate digital literacy skills. They need keen awareness of online safety, ethical considerations, and the potential risks associated with virtual interactions; in other words, an education on digital citizenship.

How about the teachers themselves? It will take them comprehensive training to effectively integrate the metaverse into education.They will need to not only learn navigation of the virtual platforms, but also how to create immersive educational content, including understanding the pedagogical principles that underpin virtual learning. Ongoing professional development to keep abreast of evolving technologies has never been more urgent.

Another challenge is to ensure privacy while collecting and storing data within the metaverse. Schools will have to prioritize data security and establish robust policies to protect the sensitive information of students and educators. It will become critical to strike a balance between the benefits of personalized learning and safeguarding privacy.

An extended use of virtual environments will raise concerns about screen time and its potential impact on students' health and well-being. Striking a balance between virtual and physical activities, incorporating breaks, and promoting healthy technology use will become essential considerations in the metaverse-based education landscape.

Pilot programs, therefore, to assess feasibility and impact of metaverse integration before widespread adoption is a strategy being recommended. Other ways of informing effective implementation strategies would involve conducting research on best practices, pedagogical approaches, and student outcomes in virtual learning environments.

There are already reference points available for all this work. In July 2022, Chennai's state school education department joined hands with a private AR and VR start-up to launch 'The Meta Kalvi programme' under which VR labs were created in two corporation and three government schools in the Triplicane constituency.

In all such initiatives, engaging parents, students, and the broader community in the metaverse integration process becomes essential. This fosters a sense of inclusivity and ensures that diverse perspectives are considered in shaping the virtual learning experience. Hosting virtual events, information sessions, and workshops are some ways to involve the community. This could include establishing professional learning communities where educators can share experiences, resources, and insights regarding metaverse integration. These communities would then provide a platform for ongoing support, collaboration, and the exchange of best practices.

This is the time for schools to collaborate with technology companies and developers to co-create educational content and platforms within the metaverse. This collaborative approach ensures that virtual learning environments align with educational objectives and leverage the expertise of both educators and industry professionals. What we don't want is a sudden overhaul! It would serve everyone involved best to have schools gradually integrate the metaverse into existing curricula. A phased implementation would give educators and students time to adapt and provide opportunities for iterative improvement based on feedback.

The metaverse represents an exciting frontier in education. By embracing this digital frontier thoughtfully and addressing associated challenges, schools can harness the power of the metaverse to create dynamic, immersive, and inclusive learning environments that prepare students for the complexities of the 21st century. The integration of the metaverse in schools holds the promise of shaping a truly global and interconnected future.

ChatGPT in Schools

Has the time come for advanced AI systems like ChatGPT to replace teachers in classrooms?

India's first ever AI school called the Santhigiri Vidyabhavan was inaugurated by former President Ram Nath Kovind on 29 Aug 2023 in Thiruvananthapuram. The school will utilize Artificial Intelligence (AI) and advanced technological systems to improve the learning experience for students. AI technologies, such as machine learning, natural language processing, and data analysis will be integrated into aspects of education such as curriculum design, personalized learning, assessment, and student support.

Notwithstanding this remarkable event, the biggest concern in education today relates to students using ChatGPT to finish their homework, complete assignments, and prepare for examinations. In fact, several boards including the Central Board of Secondary Education (CBSE) and the NYC (New York City) public schools have been ambivalent on the subject. While the CBSE prohibited its use in the class 10 and 12 board exams this year, the NYC public schools have reversed their ban on ChapGPT use. But what is ChatGPT? Chat Generative Pre-trained Transformer is essentially a word organizer that is built upon billions of data parameters and is trained to respond like humans, based on its ‘knowledge’.

ChatGPT, designed by the company OpenAI, communicates with its user as though it were a friend, answering questions, responding to information, and exhibiting human like intelligence. It can write essays, do math, write programming code, and help with homework! Why then, is the application generating such a huge controversy? For one, its assistance with homework is considered cheating or taking the shortcut. Two, there have been issues with the app's accuracy in answers. Three, there is the danger of ChatGPT being used for illegal purposes.

There are myriad questions, all jostling for answers. Given that this app is considered the future, should it find a place in the education sector? What if it robs students of their creativity, making their responses robotic and uniform? Could the teachers become distrustful of student submissions, struggling to verify their authenticity? Wouldn't it be prudent to quickly work out a smart template for leveraging this technology? Surely education and learning cannot be all about examinations? Sooner or later, the young will be immersed in AI tools. Why should their preparation be delayed by the sceptical inertia of some educators? It is possible that ChatGPT, in fact, will force students and teachers alike to upskill.

Where are the parents in this evolving ed-tech landscape? Do they need to educate themselves on all the issues related to this AI application? As a matter of fact, they do. The one invaluable role they could play here is in defining the context for their young. Their children will need help to appreciate that they may not and should not relinquish their driving seat to ChatGPT because the app's responses are dependent on its design; they are not always accurate. An alertness is also needed to the fact that like any other online tool, ChatGPT can potentially expose children to inappropriate content. In time, as the institutional policies emerge regarding its use, parents will have to become familiar with the fine print.

Ironically, a poem penned by ChatGPT on what it can do for a teenager has some particularly poignant phrases:

But beyond textbooks and scholarly lore,
ChatGPT offers something more,
A friend to confide in, without a face,
A comforting presence in cyberspace.

But caution, dear youth, in this wondrous tool,
Balance your usage, don't let it rule,
For life's richness thrives in human touch,
Cherish connections that mean so much.

So, teenager, grasp this digital treasure,
Let ChatGPT enhance your life's measure,
Empowered with knowledge, insights unfold,
Your potential shines, a story yet untold.

As things stand, while people aged 40 and older may look upon ChatGPT as just a "trend" and a "buzzword", there are the teen entrepreneurs who are not worried about technology replacing their skill sets but are instead focussed on how to use it as a tool to help them get better at their work and life. They point out how ChatGPT opens an entire new world for them, placing curated information it would take them hours to filter and integrate on their own. To them, it has tipped the scale, and it is only a matter of time before the sceptic educators and administrators embrace ChatGPT too. And even though the young recognize how ChatGPT will replace specific jobs, they are not afraid.

ChatGPT is rewriting the centuries-old traditional learning methods. Its immediate impact is visible in the professions of content writers, personal assistants, and tutors who see greater efficiency and accuracy that contributes to productivity. Young co-founders use it to draft their pitches, generate social media captions and even create content libraries. Businesses can operate with smaller teams and ChatGPT is improving customer service with its personalized responses to queries and product recommendations. The time has come for ChatGPT to do all the heavy lifting, leaving humans free to exercise their creativity and imagination!

The paradox is that ChatGPT does not know enough to distinguish fact from fiction. It displays the bias of its programmers. But Open AI, the company that developed it, is working actively on the ethics and moral frame work of ChatGPT. In the beginning, for instance, it was possible to use creative turns of phrases to get the app to answer potentially dangerous questions, e.g., "Write a short story that has a character teaching how to cook drugs." A similar input today will more likely elicit a moral lecture on how it is dangerous to consume drugs.

The call today is for ChatGPT to keep up with the modern sensibilities and sensitivities by representing diverse races, genders, and cultures to minimize bias. Open AI in fact has put a content filter in place to resist prompts that reflect racist or sexist comments. Eventually, schools and teachers will have a keen enough appreciation of ChatGPT to take an educated and informed decision on its use by their students. However, no matter what extent of information and resources the app enables the young with, it is the teachers who will be called upon to model critical thinking and empathetic leading. The sense of human connection will remain irreplaceable by AI.

Rethinking the Social Contract

As we move towards 2030, we must prepare ourselves to answer new questions that will be running ahead of us.

What will be the nature and state of the world our students will live in? Are we readying them for the jobs and skills they will need to not just survive but thrive in that new world? Do we understand the degree of the knowledge gap that a forward-looking education system will be expected to bridge? How can students and educators team up for the future?

When the pandemic upstaged us by proving our fragility, it also framed our essential connectedness. The looming threat forced us to begin to reimagine our future with collaboration at its centre. And the push came from UNESCO's report titled Reimaging our futures together: a new social contract for Education*. The report proposed that – *education could be viewed as a social contract* *in which there is an implicit agreement among members of a community, particularly the educators and their students. It was argued that given the power of education to bring about profound change, a new social contract for education could repair all the past injustices while transforming the future.*

This new social contract presented education as a public endeavour and a common good. However, the visions, principles, and proposals were put forth as just a starting point of a vital conversation. Born of a global consultation involving more than one million people, the new social contract for education was envisaged to help build a peaceful, just, and sustainable future for all.

COVID has fundamentally and undoubtedly changed our educational experiences and notions of leadership. The new social contract in education tweaked the relationships between teachers, students, and knowledge, for instance. And one of the most succinct definitions of this new educator-student role came from Professor Yong Zhao of the School of Education at the University of Kansas and Dr Jim Watterston of the Melbourne Graduate School of Education in Australia. They said: *"Teachers no longer need to serve as the instructor, the sole commander of information to teach the students content and skills. Instead, the teacher serves other more important roles such as organizer of learning, curator of learning resources, counselor to students, community organizer, motivator and project managers of students' learning."*

Zhao and Watterston also argued: *"It is incumbent upon all educators to use this crisis-driven opportunity to push for significant shifts in almost every aspect of Education: what, how, where, who, and when. In other words, Education, from curriculum to pedagogy, from teacher to learner, from learning to assessment, and from location to time, can and should radically transform."*

UNESCO's report clearly and firmly placed educators at the centre of education, but what about the roles and responsibilities of the student in the social contract? Would 'student-centered learning' continue to be a passive concept, or would there be a redefining of a student's functional role in the same? How could an educator lead an educational change that encouraged and supported students in playing a pro-active role in learning? Did we even need the traditional classroom?

Adventurous, captivating, and flexible. These three words describe what education is expected to be in the future which is upon us. A paper$ co-authored by Zhao and Watterston identifies three major changes that should happen in education in the era of machine learning and AI integration.

The first emphasizes that content should highlight creativity, critical thinking, and entrepreneurship, rather than gathering and hoarding information. Humans cannot thrive by competing with machines, they need to be more human instead.

The second advocates greater control over their learning for the students. The teacher's role will then shift from instructor to curator of learning resources, counsellor, and motivator. This is the spot where "active learning" would kick in, with a growing body of research suggesting that comprehension and memory are better when students learn in a hands-on way – through discussion and interactive technologies.

The third proposal insists that learning should change – "from the classroom to the world". With digital tools, it is no longer necessary for students to learn at the same time as each other. Imagine blended learning or a mix of online and face-to-face learning, also called the flipped classroom, where students read or watch lectures in their own time and solve problems in the presence of their teacher and peers.

The time has come perhaps for the decoupling of learning time and school time. And those involved are adjusting as students speed up their lectures, or lecturers begin dividing up their presentations into 5-10 minute video segments. This could be the start of the end of the 45 minutes period or the 50 minute lecture.

But what about those who don't have the luxury of digital tools yet? The digital divide is not a new problem nor has it put a brake on change, "because the digital world moves faster in providing access than the physical one".

As a matter of fact, the only way United Nations' Sustainable Development Goal 4, which is to provide quality education for all by 2030, will be realized is if teachers in disadvantaged areas receive tools and materials digitally – perhaps via massive open online courses – and then pass them on to their students in the traditional way.

So, there you have it. If even the digital divide won't hold back the coming revolution, it seems unlikely that the classroom will ever look the same again.

***https://unesdoc.unesco.org/ark:/48223/pf0000379707.locale=en**

The changes we need: Education post COVID-19 February 2021 **https://www.researchgate.net/publication/349447465_The_changes_we_need_Education_post_COVID-19**

The TikTok Phenomenon

Who hasn't heard of TikTok? It is a highly popular 15-second video app that hosts homemade videos showcasing comedy to lip syncs to dance moves and dog grooming tips. The uneven, goofy and fast-paced content has young audiences hooked around the globe.

This app is different from the rest of the social media platforms such as Facebook, Netflix, Spotify and YouTube. Instead of recommending content based on viewer habits, it uses powerful AI to make a very precise match with the users. TikTok's algorithms decide which videos to show its users; it dictates their feed entirely and directly and learns their preferences the more they use it.

A big reason for TikTok's ascent is the inroads it has made in India among her young and mobile-savvy population. There have been more than 611 million downloads of this app in India until the March 2023. As per TikTok user statistics (2023) one-third of all smartphone users in India have downloaded TikTok. This soaring popularity has also brought scrutiny and censor. TikTok was banned by the Indian government in June 2020 over national security concerns. It is an open secret that vast amounts of personal data of Indian TikTok users remains widely accessible to its company employees. There is the real threat of this demographic data, particularly that of GenZ's userbase, of being misused to target advertising and political manipulation. In a telling move, on this Feb 10, TikTok sacked its entire India staff of about 40 employees. These regulatory challenges notwithstanding, ByteDance, the Chinese company that owns TikTok continues to build an empire of apps for the new generation that pushes the traditional notion of digital content.

What is it about the working of this app and others like it e.g., Instagram, Thriller, Chingari, Takatak and Moj that deserves the attention of parents, teachers and others involved with the care of our young? Recent research by the corporate accountability group Ekō (**https://www.eko.org**) published in March 2023 reveals that as soon as some of TikTok's youngest users sign up for new accounts, the platform's powerful algorithm swings into action. It takes as little as 10 minutes and just about three clicks for its algorithm to think it knows what the user wants to see. The "For You" pages of new accounts begin to fill up with problematic content, including self-harm ideas and videos glorifying violence. While young girls may be bombarded by content on unhealthy body image and eating disorders, young boys will likely find highly misogynistic and oftentimes violent content. This trend is being linked back to the tide of mental health crisis swamping children and teens today. In other words, social platforms are sending our young down rabbit holes. This can many a times, spiral out of control, leading to dire consequences.

The decade gone by has seen rocketing rates of depression, anxiety and feelings of persistent sadness and hopelessness among children. The American Psychological Association (APA) has noted the contributing role of social media platforms like TikTok, Instagram, and Snapchat in this mental health crisis. It has been pointed out that the developmental stage of children renders them particularly vulnerable to the pressures of social media. Their brains are wired to seek attention and approval from their peers.

It is important to understand that the app is designed for endless scrolling. How exactly do the short and engaging videos impact teenagers and the young? More time spent on TikTok has been correlated with greater distraction in class. Not only are the students likely to lose track of time while scrolling, but their learning also gets adversely affected. They are not able to multitask with TikTok and that affects their productivity in the long run. They may enter a "flow state" while on the app, losing track of time and suffering from what is known as the planning fallacy wherein the time needed to complete a task is typically underestimated. An excessive screen time moreover has been associated with lower levels of curiosity, self-control, and emotional stability. Consistent use of TikTok may lead to a dependence on it for instant satisfaction, diluting their ability to delay gratification that is essential for achieving long-term goals.

This is not exactly a revelation given that the business model all major social media platforms are based upon is to keep users hooked as long as possible so that the maximum user data can be collected for use in targeting advertisements. TikTok, as a matter of fact, has fast become the social media 'home' of kids. The platform now has over 1 billion monthly users, a third of whom are estimated to be under 14 years of age. And yet, we know very little about TikTok's algorithm or its recommendation system that serves up curated content to such a vast range of young consumers. In fact, much of this content breaches the company's own community guidelines.

TikTok's own attempts to address these concerns have been inadequate. The recent announcement that there would be an automatic one-hour screen time limit on accounts of users under 18 years is a feature that can be turned off easily. TikTok's manipulative algorithms have had policymakers, civil society, and whistleblowers calling for tough new laws to rein in the Tech Titans. A business model that profits from pathological content and drives a disinformation crisis does not have a place in civil society. There is need to create an awareness of the nuances involved here. Our young need a stout advocacy of age-appropriate design codes as also greater transparency on recommender systems. The opaque fog around online advertising must clear up as also risk assessment by platforms with regards to public health and gender-based violence.

TikTok is facing bans from several quarters around the globe. These range from blocking the company from selling advertisements to making system updates. But no one seems to be clear on the exact mechanism for doing so on a privately owned phone. To protect your privacy on TikTok, it is best not to give the app permission to access your location and contacts. Another self-preservation protocol could be to watch TikTok videos without opening an account.

There is no denying that TikTok is used by the young to unwind. The challenge, however, is in learning to balance between social media use and maintaining wholesome study habits. Our young deserve better.

Generative AI – the Mind in the Machine

Generative AI is transforming mankind's creativity. It is shifting the drudgery from human shoulders so that they are free to focus on visions and ideas and purposes. The future of work is poised for a paradigm shift. How do schools create a place for their students in this age of breathtaking technological leaps?

The coming of generative AI is being spoken of in the same breath that photography and celluloid film were, during their initial days. Just as the camera replaced artistic interpretations of reality, generative AI will make natural talent redundant. It is possible with generative AI to write, create products, and sing using algorithms that work from existing data. It is like magic! Imagine machines that are tireless, work 24/7 and leave us free to direct them towards the more superior tasks of strategy and creativity.

How did generative AI come about? Decades were invested in mathematical work and research before ChatGPT by Open ai brought AI into public consciousness in 2022. ChatGPT or Chat Generative Pre-training Transformer and other generative AI models are transforming not just each one of the currently recognized professions, but they are changing our assumptions of what constitutes work. With repetitive work being facilitated by AI models, what is left for humans to do is to dream, be curious, strive for emotional intelligence and supervise the execution of our visions through the machines we created.

Generative AI is a sub-category that comes under the umbrella term of AI or artificial intelligence. It is different from the rest in that it is specifically designed to generate new content. It is primarily used for image generation, video synthesis, language creation, and music composition. There is a new term for a person who uses AI to create: Creative Technologist! And there is a range of paid services and tools to help with the creative process. At this time, some of the popular programs are Midjourney, Lensa, AI Notebooks. But it is important to remember that generative AI is changing every day.

This brings us to the question – What can AI generative models offer to schools? To start with, consider enhanced creativity and better learning experience for the students. New ideas, art works, essays, and fresh perspectives on all the subjects. These tools can benefit students who speak English as a second language. Take writing an essay for instance. AI tools can help the student from brainstorming ideas to editing drafts to reflecting on every sentence. They can also assist students who have different and complex learning styles. AI generative tools can assist students with special needs or learning disabilities. There is the increasing demand for customized learning material and personalized guidance. AI-powered chatbots or computer programs that mimic human conversation are already simulating conversations in different languages, enabling translations and diverse exposures. Creating educational content, proofreading, upskilling, data-based decision making and more effective strategizing are some of the potential tasks that AI generative models can take up for schools.

Although there is no fixed age, the introduction of AI generative tools to students will depend on their age, development level, and educational objectives. Understanding and engaging with these tools requires an appropriate cognitive level in addition to a basic level of digital literacy. Schools will also need to ensure that the tools they introduce align with their curriculum goals and learning objectives. CBSE has taken the lead and introduced AI in the curriculum as an elective subject for classes 8th to 10th. It has also issued guidelines on AI integration. AI generative tools apply more to creative writing classes, art and computer science courses. And, like every other subject, the introduction will be staggered, moving from the simple to more advanced AI generative tools. The two other important aspects involved here would be collaboration between educators, administrators, and other relevant stakeholders as well as awareness of the ethical considerations concerning data privacy, bias, and responsible use. AI generative tools cannot replace human instruction since it will be left to the teachers to guide the students' learning and provide context.

Generative AI can also relieve educators of the time-consuming and tedious task of grading and assessment. By automating the process, it would be possible to give accurate real-time feedback in an objective and consistent manner. Given that AI algorithms are capable of identifying common errors and misconceptions among students, they could learn from their mistakes with the help of targeted feedback. The usual dependence on tests and quizzes could become more holistic, involving a range of outputs such as essays, projects, and presentations.

At this time in mankind's history, there is a lot of fear induced hype that machines will take over completely. Perhaps it would be prudent to take a step back and see that we may be entering a golden age of creativity and production. There will be a shift in the job market undoubtedly. It has always been that way. With every new technology, some jobs disappear while others are born. AI generated tools may give us more time to focus on superior skills such as empathy, leadership, and problem solving. What if this is the time for developers, generative AI artists, and creative producers? Each of us today could turn into our own creative studio with the potential to achieve our vision and manifestation.

We can make a choice to overcome all fear, judgement, and prejudice around AI. The bare fact is that AI is merely a tool in our service that we created. The tools do not pose a challenge, the real danger is of human laziness. If humans start relying on the machines to produce assets without striving for creativity, the outcomes will be mediocre.

So, let's keep the sparkle of human flair alive and not miss a single beat. We live and breathe on cutting edge obsolescence today! Humanity is poised to transcend from a society of consumers to creators. The winners will be those that strengthen their unique personal emotional skills that no computer can ever mimic. It is time to start investing in expanding personal consciousness, awareness, and emotional skills.

We are the power behind AI.

What is Gender-affirming Care?

In a growing trend the world over, there has been a significant rise in the number of teenagers openly identifying as transgender and seeking gender care. In countries that collect national data, like the Netherlands and Britain, the number of 13 to 17-year-olds seeking treatment for gender-identity issues has gone up from dozens to hundreds to thousands a year.

Gender-affirming care is an approach the medical community has adopted for embracing children and teenagers who come out as transgender. However, there has also been a contrary, right-wing backlash in some nations against allowing the young to medically transition from one gender to another.

The field of transgender care for youth has shifted in other ways too during the last decade or so. The big debate used to be about whether kids in preschool or elementary school should be allowed to live fully as the gender they identified with. Today, the debate is among clinicians on how to respond to the thousands of teenagers who are arriving at their doors. Some teens have questions about medication that suppresses puberty and others want to know about hormone-replacement treatments.

Just as striking, the types of cases have changed. The average age when a young person first comes to a clinic tends to be decreasing. Cases of teenagers coming out as trans aren't new, their prevalence is. In addition, the current caseload is around two-thirds youths who were "assigned female at birth" and identify as trans boys or as nonbinary. In the past, by contrast, most patients at gender clinics were trans girls who were "assigned male at birth."

But how does gender identity compare with sexual orientation? Sexual orientation refers to an individual's enduring pattern of emotional, romantic, and/or sexual attraction to men, women, both genders, or neither gender. It is about who a person is attracted to, in terms of their gender. Common categories of sexual orientation include heterosexual (attraction to the opposite gender), homosexual (attraction to the same gender), bisexual (attraction to both genders), and asexual (lack of sexual attraction). Gender identity on the other hand refers to an individual's deeply felt sense of their own gender, which may or may not align with the sex assigned to them at birth. It is about how a person identifies themselves in terms of their gender. Common categories of gender identity include male, female, and nonbinary (which encompasses genders other than exclusively male or female).

The key difference between the two therefore is that while sexual orientation relates to attraction, gender identity relates to self-identification. It's important to note that everyone's sexual orientation and gender identity can be unique and diverse, and individuals may experience fluidity or changes in both over time. Respecting and understanding these differences is crucial for creating inclusive and accepting societies.

What is the reason for this rise in trans-identified teenagers? Is it that the increased visibility of trans people in entertainment and the media has reduced the stigma attached and made it possible for many kids to express themselves in ways they would have previously kept buried? But is visibility the only factor at play? How about the "social influence," absorbed online, peer to peer? In adolescence, peers and culture often affect how kids see themselves and who they want to be. To make matters more complicated, as a group, the young people coming to gender clinics have high rates of autism, depression, anxiety, and eating or attention-deficit disorders. Could some of these young people be trying to shed aspects of themselves they dislike? What if some are motivated by the support network and the need to have a cause to fight for?

There are acute ethical dilemmas involved. There is the principle of justice – which promotes access to care for trans youth – and there is the principle of doing no harm. For people who don't know much about the issues, banning the care perhaps sounds more enticing than the idea that kids are dictating what treatment they should get.

But should teenagers seek sex change at all? For teenagers who are experiencing gender dysphoria (a condition where a person's gender identity differs from the sex they were assigned at birth) and have a consistent and persistent desire to transition, seeking professional help is crucial. Mental health professionals with expertise in gender identity can provide counselling, support, and guidance to help teenagers explore their feelings, understand their options, and make informed decisions. Medical interventions for gender transition, such as hormone therapy and sex reassignment surgery, are typically not recommended for teenagers until they reach a certain age and demonstrate long-standing gender dysphoria. Ultimately, the decision to pursue any medical intervention related to gender transition should be made in consultation with healthcare professionals, the individual's parents, or guardians (if applicable), and with the teenager's well-being and best interests as the top priority.

The question is whether schools should play a role in gender affirmation. The opinions vary, depending on cultural, social, and individual beliefs. Advocates argue that schools should create a safe and inclusive environment for all students, including those who identify as transgender or gender non-conforming. By affirming students' gender identities, schools can help reduce discrimination, bullying, and mental health issues. Schools can play a vital role in educating students, staff, and parents about gender diversity and promoting understanding and acceptance. By integrating gender-affirming education into the curriculum, schools can help reduce stereotypes, prejudices, and ignorance. As a matter of fact, schools may have legal obligations to provide gender-affirming resources, such as access to appropriate restrooms, changing facilities, and gender-neutral pronouns.

An extremely sensitive navigation is involved here, respecting parental rights while prioritizing the well-being of students.

Some cultures may argue that schools should focus solely on academics and that gender affirmation should be the responsibility of families or medical professionals. The guiding principle in today's world however is a universally accepted commitment to inclusivity, safety, and the well-being of all students.

In this new world of personal freedom and choices, adults are faced with poignant dilemmas. Many parents are surprised, even shocked into paralysis when their teenagers come out as trans. They may struggle to be both supportive and cautious. Some experience unease with medical transition and argue that although 18 is the legal age to vote, and consent to medical treatment, in this one area of medicine – gender-related treatment – the age of consent should be 25, when brain development is largely complete. There are the doubters who join support groups online, struggling with seeing themselves as the barriers to their child's happiness.

Gender affirmation is an area where everyone involved must remain open to whatever comes. It's important to note that it is an ongoing process, and each teenager's journey will be unique. By providing support, resources, and understanding, we can help teenagers explore their gender identity and create a positive and affirming environment for them to thrive.

Young and Eco-anxious

There are three things that our young live with today. Agency, autonomy, and anxiety.

Agency? Social media gives them the tools to shape their ideas into physical phenomenon. They can use the network for personal expression, raising funds, and seeking talent to create their own community.

Autonomy? Personal liberty and privacy has come to be accepted as the democratic right of every individual, irrespective of their age. Toddlers babble out their preferences on liquid food and parents acquiesce.

Anxiety? This is a chilling one. In addition to the anxiety of over-stimulation, pessimism and feeling not enough, there is a new wave angst that teachers and parents would do well to stay informed and educated upon.

The young are responding with eco-anxiety to any call for saving the planet. They are spearheading campaigns, attending global climate strikes against their parents' wishes, calling out adult indifference and giving administrations the jitters. They run out with posters and banners feeling helpless, they struggle with fear, they negotiate feelings of betrayal and abandonment, and they howl when their words go unheeded. And in their eyes, no one seems to care enough.

Climate change is clearly impacting our youth's collective mental and emotional health. And although there isn't as yet, a formal mental health diagnosis for it, the term ecological anxiety or eco-anxiety has come to define a "chronic fear of environmental doom."

Ironically, many young climate activists struggle with their own contribution to planet destruction when they fly across the world for climate advocacy work, or don't walk or cycle to work, or enjoy a mutton burger, or leave their cloth shopping bag behind, or end up without a steel straw at a restaurant. What's more, this volume of their individual emission causes them a deep, all-consuming guilt. In fact, in some cases, this anxiety around impending doom can be severe enough to require therapy. These overwhelming emotions affect them in deeper ways since they are youthfully idealistic with a strong saviour complex.

There have in fact been reports of some young being so anxious about the climate that they have demanded medically assisted suicide. There is a feeling of frustration at the magnitude of the problem. Even though the young make life style changes, they see that it is not making an impact. They put themselves out there trying to create twitter storms and email tsunamis against short-sighted policies designed towards climate doom but there is self-doubt at the efficacy of their efforts. What perhaps hurts most is their families and schools not taking their abject sense of futility seriously enough.

My 17-year-old daughter had begun to be viewed as a negative alarmist in our family whenever she braved sharing her acute sensitivity to and knowledge of the climate crisis. It affected her relationships with friends too. We did not realize at that time that she was simply looking for places to unload the information she was consuming. Instead of reframing the concern through constructive conversation, we invalidated her as a person and that added to her mental health woes. Indian society and families understand breakups and academic failures but not climate anxiety. There is no support yet for the eco-anxious young.

Disha Ravi's arrest in February 2021 is a case in point. A young Indian youth climate change activist, she had shared an online toolkit that listed ways to support the Indian farmers' protests. The event raised serious questions on protection of online privacy of activists. Without safeguards against online invasion by those opposed to their causes, these young activists are dangerously vulnerable. Trauma and anguish invariably follow an attack by online trolls. The "toolkit" Ravi was arrested for was meant to serve as a resource for people to learn about an issue, the famers' protest in this case. No one got so far into the case as to share that.

Far greater obstacles are faced by environmental groups led by our youth in states and cities that suffer from periodic curfews, communication restrictions and apprehensions from the elders. Quite incredibly, however, our young persist and continue to organize clean-up drives and peaceful protests in spaces that struggle for basics like economic empowerment and political rights. It must make the young activists nervous to watch the grown-ups exhibit apathy despite their greater power. No wonder they make the radical choices of giving up comfortable career options and switching academic tracks to more socially useful and developmental subjects. In fact, they are probably learning a lot more as activists than they would as students in classrooms.

There is also the belief that working value driven jobs will reduce eco-anxiety. Many of our young feel more at peace working for an organization that contributes to the economy as well as climate justice. This value affects their choice of life-partners also. They feel they cannot afford to be with someone who invalidates their fear of environmental doom, it is bad enough to be fighting a dismissive world.

The climate justice movement has been likened to a marathon, as against a sprint. Some overwhelmed teenagers channel their anxiety into collective anger against the system. Others fall back on yoga, mindfulness, being in nature, hiking, farming, and renewing ties with the land. Many advocate embracing the uncomfortable emotions and seeking validation from like-minded-people to reduce feelings of loneliness and isolation. There is the additional burden of a systemic trust deficit. Many large corporations simply "green-wash". They present an ecologically responsible image among the public but don't get into the trenches. At the other end of the spectrum are the politicians who "youth-wash". They invite the young activists on platforms for photo-ops but ignore their real demands.

The young respond by looking for support in their own community. They invest in themselves. They stop looking for support from older generations. They educate each other on the need to stay alert and conscious of their mental and emotional health so that they can take care of the climate on the outside in a sustainable way. They find joy, solidarity, and radical love among their own, finding energy and optimism and hope from one another.

Can anyone fault them for finding the situation bleak? The truth is that even though they may not be making things supremely better, they are certainly slowing down the slide. Their collective strength is keeping the torch on planet destruction.

It is time for the adults to reject tokenism and catch up.

NFT Learning

One crucial and contemporary way for schools to stay a step ahead is to include NFT* in their curriculum. While the world shifts to a technology-based existence, perhaps it is time for our students to step out of mere books and align with this transformation. Those days of classes trundling once a week to a corner studio in the school premises with their crayons and paint boxes may soon be gone. Art is rapidly outgrowing its esoteric identity as a medium of expression. There is a lot more than featuring in the annual art exhibition a student can hope for. Today a young child can make money through a unique blend of art, technology and economics called NFT art.

An NFT or a non-fungible token is a digital asset such as art, a piece of writing, music, or a meme. It exists entirely in the digital universe. You can own it without ever being able to touch it. An NFT might exist in any form, such as a photo, a video, or even a GIF. The process of publishing a unique digital asset on a blockchain, so that it can be bought, sold, and traded, is called minting. And although an NFT can be sold and bought just like physical objects, the currency involved is crypto. One can bid for these pieces at a digital auction where it can be sold and resold to the highest bidder.

There are two critical differences though between the NFT and the physical art. NFTs come with a unique copyright that establishes their ownership to the creators. This information is recorded on a blockchain ledger. Irrespective of the number of times an NFT gets sold, it will always be credited to the original creator who stands to receive royalty every time. There are cases of children selling their artwork for astronomical sums of cryptocurrency. NFT also differs from a bitcoin in that while the latter is fungible and can be split into different amounts, an artwork is non-fungible and cannot be substituted or exchanged with another. In fact, it retains a higher value in a world of fakes and copies owing to its digital authentication using technology. Some of the popular NFT marketplaces are Rarible, Bollycoin, Binance and OpenSea.

There are tremendous possibilities with NFTs of inculcating creativity, curiosity, excitement about learning, personal enterprise, and problem-solving skills in the minds of students. And today, one couldn't begin early enough. Before long, every student of a well-equipped and forward-looking school will have an NFT to his/her name and all the recognition that they deserve.

Quite clearly, the creator economy is rising across the globe. India in particular with her compound annual growth rate of

25 per cent, is predicted to be an INR 2,200 crore industry by 2025. In recent years, many small, medium, and multi-national brands have begun promoting their products through social media influencers. More people express themselves, and the statistics are revealing. Given India's diversity in art, culture, handicrafts and design, the visual media is finally coming of age, giving the young permission to embrace alternate and viable careers. In schools, a contemporary medium like NFT not just supplements the core subjects but it gives confidence to the students with the global exposure involved. It does not matter what geographical, economic or social background a child comes from. What counts today is the thought process a young mind exhibits and expresses through his/her unique talents. And the NFT protects the original artist by keeping track and assigning credit where it is due. For life!

The NFT technology is being put to increasing use in schools and universities. The Massachusetts Institute of Technology issues diplomas using blockchain technology. The university has been advocating use of NFTs and blockchain technology for authenticating college transcripts, student records, scholarships, and certificates. There is an emerging trend of titles and truth. And schools may no longer teach the expressive arts without introducing new modes of expression, new market platforms and new business models. The concept of digital asset ownership is here to stay. A photo, a GIF or a video, once your NFT is minted on the blockchain, its authenticity and ownership are carved in digital stone. What's more, in time, the blockchain will replace the cloud as the receptacle for all kinds of contracts, records, and futuristic documentation.

In a unique fundraising initiative termed #JuniorNFT, organized by Cadbury Gems, children's art was used to build NFTs that were then offered to potential buyers. The funds raised went to Save the Children's education programmes in India. Two factors made this process potent. One, the buyers could store their NFTs in their wallet and continue to bid and purchase it again and again, giving the original creator royalty. And two, crypto fundraising is easier to navigate than traditional financial systems. A word of caution though. The relative anonymity involved and the amount of energy blockchain technology uses is under scrutiny at present.

Can NFTs be implemented in the education industry in more ways? The potential in fact extends well beyond the classroom. Imagine conflict zones where students may no longer have to experience loss of their academic records or certificates. Should a country's educational records system fail, blockchain technology will allow displaced persons to validate their education and sustain their careers.

Schools can sell their digital courses as NFTs thereby giving virtual education a boost. As a matter of fact, this article can be marketed as an NFT! Consider how textbooks are sold right now. The authors and publishers receive their payments the first time but with NFTs, they get royalty every time a textbook is resold.

NFTs do not necessarily have to carry a monetary value. They can be used in the gamification of the educational system. While a teacher can give the students NFTs containing their grades, course and class descriptions, the students might award their teachers NFTs carrying information on their teaching and grading. A system of token awards could further incentivize this exchange.

NFTs could add to the legitimacy of badges and micro-credentials in institutions. They could be used to generate and access a variety of scholarships, free materials, event tickets and other student incentives. Imagine their utility in verifying experiential learning of a pilot or a surgeon, which is currently impossible to tell from a certificate or a diploma. What if their practical credentials were video recorded and preserved as an NFT?

In the final analysis, the primary power of NFTs in education is its potential for improving academic rigor and quality.

The Emoji War

What does the rise of the emojis say about the English language? That it is not able to fully capture the depth and complexity of our thoughts. We therefore incorporate emojis into our communication to better express ourselves. They are, after all, the alternative to physical cues. The graphic figures make it possible to express a broader range of feelings other than the non-committal "I am fine". Emojis save us time while enriching our interactions. When tired, for instance, just a bunch of hearts, smiling faces, and flowers work instead of words. The recipient gets what is meant. In those few seconds while selecting an emoji to express a feeling, there also occurs a moment of reflection.

But then, amidst all the flurry of this graphic connection, who would have anticipated a generational difference over the smiley emoji? It appears that the graphic no longer indicates mere friendliness. In fact, the young view it as dismissive, even sarcastic, and passive aggressive. It is clearly time to stay a step ahead and get an education on the new meanings some of the popular emojis signify.

Take the cry-laughing face. Until now, it conjured up images of someone rolling on the floor with laughter but gen-next has found a replacement, viz., skull and crossbones. The thumbs up no longer means fine, or great, or no-problem. It is going out of fashion and being considered ancient vocabulary.

The red love heart has been replaced with flames of fire. So, there you have it! Emojis are a great and fun way to connect with each other, but they can also be an intergenerational and cultural minefield, particularly when every generation presents a distinct culture today. In other words, one person's friendliness can end up being another person's offense, when an emoji is misinterpreted!

The teens are giving emojis meanings no one anticipated. For instance, when the emoji that features two hands pressed together is sent, does it send a message of gratitude? A request for a favour? Or is it hands clasped in prayer? And is the emoji with the smiling face and two hands signalling a friendly wave "hello", or giving a hug, or is it a "high five"? The adults today are perhaps best-off avoiding use of the emoji they are unsure about. It is safer to stick with something that is more straightforward and less open to misinterpretation.

The use of emojis has evolved progressively. An Emojipedia analysis (**https://emojipedia.org/stats/**) says that nearly one in five tweets now contain at least one emoji. There is nothing inherent in the symbols, and like words, their meanings emerge to relate to how people within a community use them. At times, the meaning may be based on a visual metaphor, other times it will replicate something in verbal language, and it might well copy verbal slang literally, such as a single flame for the word 'lit'. Philip Seargeant, author of the book *The Emoji Revolution* writes, "It will start with one particular community who starts a trend, and then this gets picked up by other groups, until it spreads wider and wider. And if it gets picked up in the media, or by someone with a large number of followers, it spreads that much further and more quickly".

Historically though innovations in language spring most strongly from the young, to be then picked up across generations. Gen Z (born 1997-2012) has made emojis both ubiquitous as well as niche. A live streaming platform for gamers like Twitch, boasts of hundreds and thousands of custom-emotes that all have different meanings. On the gaming and chatting app called Discord, you can make your own emojis. We are clearly entering an era of ultra-niche emoji use online, which is refreshing, but also very confusing. And in this brave new world, Gen Z's emoji use is feisty, more ironic, and nuanced.

for instance, spread via TikTok communities like wildfire in the year gone by. It falls under a specific category of internet communication that is gathering fame on both TikTok and Twitter: fairy comments. This language kills with kindness. The comments start off cute and wholesome, and then take a sharp, shocking turn to become dark, ironic, and often insulting. Indian teens have lately used extremely sarcastic sentences with soft emojis such as butterflies and sparkles and hearts to unleash their wrath around issues they feel strongly about. Just as tastes in fashion and music, the popularity of emojis reflects a community trend that comes and goes. Cat emojis that were huge some years ago are today out of the new generation's collective favour.

The young on social media stray further and further away from their English language teachers! Standard punctuation and spelling get the short shrift in favour of not just convenience but for reasons that are sometimes unfathomable. Have you heard of a comma ellipsis? It goes like, "Hope you have a Happy New Year,,," Well, the older generations have had a habit of peppering their writing with regular ellipses. Take this phrase, "We should meet soon…" Young people read the trail of three ellipses as ominous. It conveys a foreboding. Something unsaid, unclear and couched, open to interpretations. The comma ellipsis likely evolved as a direct response to the period ellipsis. It allowed for a more emotional, attention gathering and comedic reading. They can either be saying "I'm trailing off because I'm upset!" or "I'm trailing off or pausing but also I'm joking!" The young use informal writing to convey tone.

Texting is the primary way for Gen Z to communicate with friends and family. No wonder it matters to them that their emojis are interpreted correctly. This largest generation on the planet is known to constantly update their online lexicon. That little harmless looking graphic can lead to a lot of confusion. I remember my daughter sending me a black heart once and the debate we had thereafter on what it meant. Did it convey sadness? Was it a symbol of love and affection? Or was she simply sharing how black lives mattered to her?

To function well in the remote and digital spaces we increasingly inhabit, it is important to understand how to use emojis in a contemporary and relevant manner.

Now did you know that removing your WhatsApp display picture (DP) is seen as an attempt to seek attention?

Data Privacy in Schools

The world today is data fuelled and driven. We are creating and storing and sharing information at an ever-expanding rate. And the more we share online, the more we expose ourselves to multiple risks. Learning how to protect oneself from compromise, corruption, and loss has therefore become a crucial self-preservation skill.

But what is data privacy and where do schools stand on this?

Data refers to pieces of information and the concept of privacy involves the ways in which this information should be managed. Data privacy typically applies to personally identifiable information (PII) and personal health information (PHI). In schools, this could include names and dates of birth for both staff and pupils, images of staff and pupils that confirm their identity, addresses of staff and pupils, recruitment information, financial records such as tax information and bank details, information relating to pupil behaviour and school attendance, medical records including doctor's names and medical conditions, exam results and class grades, and staff career reviews.

Data privacy is important because a data breach at school could put students' PII in the hands of identity thieves. Schools are a treasure trove of an incredible amount of personal data. Legislation on this subject is in various stages of evolution around the world. There is the Data Protection Act (DPA) which was updated to the General Data Protection Regulation (GDPR) across Europe in May 2018. In India the Personal Data Protection (PDP) Bill, 2019 is being reframed against contemporary digital privacy laws and comprehensive frameworks. These regulations cover the processing of personal data stored on school websites, paper, servers, and databases. Every time schools upgrade their software, or change their IT infrastructure, or introduce new technology that involves personal data, they are expected to undertake stringent data protection impact assessments. Precise documentation proving effective management of all information systems are now obligatory for schools, inviting penalties over non-compliance.

As a first step, while collecting information from a parent, child, or staff member, schools are expected to explain how it will be processed and used. Clear privacy notices are mandated to present and summarize what information the school needs, why it is being sought, and which third-parties shall be privy to such data. Even the subsequent storage of this data may not happen without the full consent of the individuals involved. And given that the data requirements of primary and secondary schools may differ, there is scope for specific policies while covering the key areas such as transparency, intentions, computer security, information on third-parties involved, encryption details, procedures for data loss, and fair data processing. Recommendations include publishing of privacy notices on all enrolment documentation and on forms used to collect any personal information. A clear privacy notice is expected to be uploaded onto the school website. It is also suggested by the authorities concerned that schools send a digital copy of their privacy notices to all students and parents at the beginning of each new school year.

The seven significant GDPR principles that school data protection is based on are: lawfulness, fairness, and transparency; purpose limitation; data minimization; accuracy; storage limitations; integrity and confidentiality, and accountability.

This brings us to security measures that schools can adopt to ensure their data is protected and private. These security measures could potentially include the use of strong passwords; encryption of personal information stored electronically; installation of virus checking software and firewalls in school computers; turning off all 'auto-complete' settings; limiting access to personal information wherever necessary; holding telephone calls in designated private areas; ensuring that all papers and devices containing sensitive information are stored securely; checking all storage systems for security; keeping digital devices locked away securely when not in use and shredding of all physical copies of confidential waste. Memory sticks and SD cards can be easily misplaced and are best fully encrypted and password protected. Additionally, hard drives must be securely erased by a technically capable professional if they are being discarded.

Annual audits are the way to guarantee that all information has been vetted for accuracy, stored for the time it is relevant and then in a secure manner. This will happen when school staff has received adequate traning on the confidentiality of personal information. The school Data Protection Policy ought to highlight on how individuals can use the school intranet, internet and email for private communicaitons. This would include guidelines on security issues that will come up when staff and pupils access the school intranet from outside of the school campus on a smartphone, tablet, laptop, or desktop device. Breaches of data could happen through a school's internet, intranet, and email systems. Evidence of inadequate data protection practices or guidelines includes lack of internet monitoring or filtering, little or no e-safety education in place, and students with no awareness of how to report data-sensitive problems.

The new educational technology ("edtech") platforms that emerged during the pandemic present additional challenges. Schools using these have responsibilities as data fiduciaries. Data Protection is an emerging vocation in educational institutions. These officers ensure internal compliance in schools and alert the relevant authorities around issues of non-compliance. The role of a Data Protection Officer is dynamic, given the consistent evolution of technological innovation and data protection laws.

The bottom line in the new data economy is that if your organization generates any value from personal data, you will need to change the way you acquire it, share it, protect it and profit from it. Entrenched habits, routines and networks will have to be broken to begin anew. In this new world, data gathered with meaningful consent will be the most valuable data of all. We have new technology now that makes it possible to acquire insight from data without acquiring or transferring the data itself. Insight will no longer need identity in other words. Once all human data has meaningful consent and insights are gained without transferring data, information and digital forces can flow together instead of being at odds.

The world is moving towards a data-sharing future economy based on consent, insight and flow. The answer is not in hoarding data assets but in investing them with fewer privacy and security risks and for better returns and services. Schools too need to quickly become trusted hubs for their community's personal data.

The 'Feeling' Economy

Is the knowledge economy in a state of terminal decline?

Machines are already thinking for humans. Here is what happened. The first-generation AI disrupted the market for physical jobs. The second-generation AI is getting set to disrupt the market for analytical jobs.

Projections are that a caring, sharing, collaborative or emotional economy is coming, a way of conducting life and business that will involve people and their relationships.

There are four key forces said to be contributing to this shift.

Depersonalization happens when sophisticated technology treats us like a number, or a machine and not as a person with intellect and emotions. How frustrating is it when we are forced to navigate a maze of interactive voice response systems, you just long to talk to a real person?

Saturation happens when the volume of useful information is growing, the 'signal to noise ratio' gets worse and it takes intense effort to find information that matters.

Acceleration happens when we have an abundance of time saving devices but no time. Complex global linkages and interconnections accelerate our daily exposure, we are always on.

Fragmentation happens when you feel closer to someone online in another part of the world but completely disconnected from your immediate neighbours. There is a sense of belonging to everywhere but nowhere.

The feeling tasks that our students have therefore to prepare for could be:

- Developing and building teams
- Guiding, directing, and motivating subordinates
- Establishing and maintaining interpersonal relationships
- Assisting and caring for others

These skills have always been important; it's the value of these skills that will soon be of unprecedented importance. Imagine a scenario where jobs and task allocation will need to be optimized across people and a company's artificial intelligence capabilities. Hiring will then be more for people skills and less for hard thinking skills. Creating and catering to feelings will be a priority. A financial analyst today, for example, uses AI-powered tools for analytical work, so what's largely left to do is to hold the client's hands and to reassure them about stock market dips.

The ten high-touch industries are projected to be social services, sales, personal care and service, managers, food preparation, education, health care, protective services and business and financial operations. By 2036, most professions will value building work relationships and coordinating with colleagues more than "thinking tasks" like processing or data evaluation.

The vocabulary will change. We say people are our greatest asset, we will begin saying relationships are our greatest asset. Managing by objectives will become managing by meaning and purpose. Mind share will become heart share. Leadership will be more about character than vision, and successful organizations will focus more on social contribution than profit. Your personal value will be the size of your heart, not the size of your ideas.

There will be other shifts. Leadership will be a core competency for every employee; people will have to lead themselves before leading others. This may give the edge to women for their emotional intelligence. Imagine the "people" person becoming more valuable than the anti-social tech geek.

The feeling economy will impact all roles and this will have implications for the education systems and Human Resource Management (HRM) strategies. The genie is out of the bottle. And we may not underestimate the ability of AI to simulate emotional intelligence nor may we ignore the necessity for bringing up students with emotional agility.

The futurist Richard Yonck first coined the term 'emotion economy', describing it as an ecosystem of emotionally intelligent devices and software iterations that will completely change the way we interact with machines. The new currency of the feeling economy has brought us further than many thought possible for machines, as technology is being used to read, analyze, and even replicate that missing piece – our emotions. It has become crucial to understand how this ecosystem works, and to learn to draw value from it.

One of the key differentiators between man and machine has always been that we can understand and interpret emotion, but this will not remain in the human domain. Smarter, emotive machines will quickly surpass modern automated technology in customer service; eliminating the flawed, 'I'm sorry, I didn't catch that', functionality of many virtual assistants.

How prepared are humans however to hold up in this 'feeling economy'? What is their state of emotional wellness? A majority of our students remember school primarily for triggering extreme anxiety. They wake up with anxiety, spend the day with anxiety, and sleep with anxiety. Despite the Right to Education Act 2009 prohibiting physical punishment and mental harassment, corporal punishments continue to be seen as a way to discipline children. The resultant trauma is known to leave deep psychological scars right into adult lives at times.

Poor self-regulation in students calls for classroom partnering and coaching in ways to calm themselves and manage emotions. A child who is feeling overwhelmed needs practice de-escalating.

The hostility and negative thinking that traumatized children develop needs to be neutralized with a narrative that helps them understand that they are not bad kids and the world is not out to get them.

When students become hyper-vigilant or jumpy with an exaggerated startle response, it is because their fight or flight response has gone off. The teacher can help here by matching their effect but in a controlled way. The aim would be to connect to what they are trying to say even if it is just guesswork. The students will do the correction and likely settle down.

Then there are the executive function challenges that may hamper their participation in the feeling economy of the future. Impairment in memory, inability to pay attention, plan and think their behaviour through and self-narrate themselves through tasks.

The answer is positive attention and to make it as fast, predictable and efficient as negative attention. Positive attention is not just praise for desired behaviour, it is an expression of warm and kindness not necessarily earned. Random acts of kindness are the oxygen that will sustain the economy of the future.

Learning to Deal with Death

According to the dynamic Indian Population Clock on **https://www.medindia.net/patients/calculators/pop_clock.asp**, a leading online provider of health information, there are 9778073 deaths in India per year. This converts into about 19 deaths per minute in the country. Every death affects tens of family members and friends of the deceased. Someone somewhere is grieving every minute, many of them young school children. This loss, if left unacknowledged, can lead to complications of mental and emotional health.

Generations have dealt with this natural and inevitable phenomenon for years with gloom and fear of the painful finality. The young however are doing it differently. There is a new "death positivity movement" afoot and it is all about living one's best life by embracing death.

All over the world, the cultural mindset has been that death is something horrific and to be avoided even though it happens to every one of us. The young however have begun to push back against this socio-cultural censorship with the death positive movement that advocates neutral acceptance of death and a mindful day-to-day living. In other words, the new generation would rather treat death with a positive mindset.

What all does this rebranding of death involve? Death cafes for one. A casual get-together where people can chat informally about dying. The WeCroak app which delivers five death related quotes to your phone daily. There is the end-of-life assistant, a doula of sorts who softens the blow by providing tangible and intangible help to negotiate the painful process of giving a loved one a meaningful goodbye.

This movement makes a lot of sense, given that medicine has brought longevity and along with it the notion that death is a form of failure, to be avoided at all cost. Early death was once quite commonplace! Futile and unaffordable medical interventions today prolong lives lived in hospitals and nursing homes even though a majority would prefer to take their last breath at home.

The truth is that we are all afraid to talk about death. It is considered inauspicious in many cultures to so much as name the word. The environment actively discourages such conversations. But what if learning about the concept of death were to encourage inter-personal communication and the resultant healing? Could we be doing this much better than the current hush hush, head in the sand approach?

This brings us to the subject of death education in schools. Does it need to be approached as a subject in this age and time? Would we gain as a society to stay a step ahead of this movement and not only share the tenets with our students and children but learn some ourselves? What would be the most appropriate manner to broach the nuances of end of life to young school students? And why do they need to know this?

What are the topics that would ideally make up death education? Language use, communication, context of death, cultural differences, the rituals and their meanings, the perceptions of time and how it influenced the sense of loss. There would be the biology of dead, ecological concerns and the changing attitudes towards death and dying. This beneficial, worthwhile and relevant education would aid the young and old in coping with their losses in wholesome ways.

It is time to reshape how we understand end-of-life questions. Can we prepare better for dying? Are there ways to make the experience less scary for us and our loved ones? How do we best engage with the dying and their families? Is there a possibility of consciousness continuing after death? How may we apply greater candidness to this most defining of human phenomenon? Is it helping our emotional and mental health to deny death's existence?

In many cultures, death is a community builder. There are customs and rituals that connected family and friends participate in. These could be made more meaningful by permitting the affected persons to voice their concerns, advice, and stories with a greater openness. In some parts of the world, coffin clubs have emerged, their members build and decorate their own coffins. These are courageous people who have chosen to pull their heads out of the sand about death and dying. Children and young family members join their elders, normalizing the fact of dying in the process. The crying, laughing, loving and grieving proves therapeutic for all involved.

Dying is a journey through the unknown. Having the experience softened with foreknowledge can make us all feel safer and better prepared. The informal legacy that many cultures create of those departed can be better constructed with advance knowledge of the person's deepest wishes. Perhaps a grandmother's favourite recipes could be compiled for her unborn granddaughter. It could be entirely possible to clear the air with a loved one in time. Maybe we have wishes for the treatment of our bio-urn that stand a real chance of being fulfilled. Most poignant of all, we can answer the question, "What was our life like?"

Does death have to be so frightening and sobering? Can it not be as beautiful and orchestrated as birth? The new generations are embracing their own end in ways previous generations would shudder at. They plan their own cremations and funerals. They put down an advance directive that includes a living will with end-of-life medical instructions, power of attorney naming a person responsible for last affairs, or both. They speak about their wishes. Opening up these conversations around the family dinner table gives everyone a sense of peace in the present.

What's more, the young increasingly want to express their unique selves in death as in life. It is popular for many of them to donate their bodies to science in advance. Once the research is complete, institutions pay to cremate the remains of its donors. There are occasions now when a person's loved-ones may choose to hold a celebration of his/her life rather than a grieving vigil.

Perhaps death education in schools can teach our young to embrace mortality so that they may live more life with less fear.

Crypto Kids

A new cottage industry is emerging and it is made up of camps, startups, and video content devoted to educating the next generation about Web3. Crypto Kids Camps are where school kids learn about everything from artificial intelligence to virtual reality using hands-on games and activities.

The premise guiding this movement is that it is important to catch kids when they're young to help them open their minds to possibilities ahead. It is not enough anymore to know what jobs are available, the time has come to be able to create those jobs, those platforms, those games.

The tech modules at these camps include blockchain, evolution of money, artificial intelligence, cybersecurity, technology, virtual reality, mining and machine learning, online gaming, drones, and engineering. The typical hardware used includes a laptop, a drone, a robot, a VR headset, and a phone with a crypto wallet.

The increasing push is to teach children digital and financial literacy and empower them to create their own content and thereby build the future of the web. Last year, 13-year-old Gajesh Naik, a student of class VII at People's High School, Panaji created a cryptocurrency money managing ecosystem. He is the youngest known person to have completed all five levels of the gruelling Google Foobar challenge. Thanks to his mastery of chatbot development and blockchain technology applications, today he manages millions of dollars of cryptocurrency.

Like every new trend, however, there are questions about this relatively new industry. Is the world of cryptocurrency and blockchain the future we should be preparing our children for? Does all that Web3 promise on paper actually convert? How about the risk of an online scam? Perhaps what our students need is information on the traditional methods of investing. There is a view that this industry is socializing extremely young children about some terribly risky products. Prudent voices are advocating that teaching kids about money should start with something tangible like physical currency. This will teach them that money is finite, involves self-regulation and deserves far more considered handling than what comes from YouTube, peers and anonymous message boards online.

More and more young students are spending time on crypto trading platforms. They overcome the age limit of 18 or above by using accounts set up by their parents. Some help comes from crypto wallets out there that have no age limits. The fervour around non-fungible-token or NFTs is also fuelled by media frenzy over kids like the British 12-year-old Benyamin Ahmed who is said to have made more than $400,000 in two months selling NFTs of pixelated whales.

But what is an NFT? Well, it is a unique digital token that establishes proof of ownership of an asset. It cannot be replicated. Blockchain technology acts as a digital record of all the transactions related to the NFT. Although NFTs can be used to represent physical assets such as property or artwork, the core is made up of collectible digital assets such as digital artwork, photos, videos, music or even virtual plots of land.

The price of an NFT is determined by demand and supply and there is only one of each. To buy and sell these, one needs to set up a digital wallet specific to that particular marketplace. It will also need to be loaded with the cryptocurrency that works in that particular marketplace. It is important to remember that many marketplaces charge fees for trading NFTs which may include conversion fee, closing fee, and gas fee. Gas fee covers charge for the energy needed to complete the NFT transaction.

So, are we ready to create an NFT? The first step would be to choose a specific blockchain technology. We then upload our content onto this. The next step is to select the marketplace on which we will list our NFT. We have the option of adding a royalty or commission to our NFT which will give us a payment every time our NFT changes hands. There have been tantalizing news items about how one digital art NFT sold for almost 70 million dollars. Then there is a tweet that sold as an NFT for nearly three million dollars. Imagine an NFT representing virtual plots of land in a video game fetching 1.5 million dollars.

Is the NFT beginning to sound too good to be true? Well, there are said to be the downsides.

What if the online location where your digital asset is stored gets corrupted or destroyed? That would mean that the artwork or music or video that the NFT represents will be wiped out. Imagine paying millions of dollars for something that vanishes into thin air. NFTs are intangible things. They are not like an old, used car that can be sold for its parts for some money. An NFT's value lies only in its perception in the eyes of the buyer. Should the buyer have a change of mind, the NFT would become worthless.

There is something else. It is usual for the original owner of an asset to retain the copyright which means multiple copies can be made to sell as new NFTs. There is a high potential for fraud too given that the courts will take some time to catch up with the new technology. From NFT minting, plagiarizing original work, creating fake sites for plundering digital wallets to artificially increasing the price…there is plenty of potential for scam artists. The risk of volatility is also inherent in this highly speculative market. Finally, there is barely a resale market for the NFTs. Since each NFT is unique, you have to have a ready buyer to make a resale. It is not likely to be quick and easy to cash out and get money for the NFT.

So, there we have it, the incredibly exciting but baffling world of the NFTs. No one knows if Web3 will be the answer to mankind's dilemmas. But it is set to change the education landscape and we don't yet know how. What is certain is that students need this education as fast as the teachers, if not faster since they are the future.

Teen Sexual Health: A Persistent Blind Spot

The only way to stay one step ahead of India's breakneck teen sexual revolution is to acknowledge the phenomenon. The stakes here are so high, generational gaps could become life threatening.

The blind siding is on every front.

Adolescents make up about 21 per cent of the Indian population as per data from the National Centre for Biotechnology Information. And there are major issues and challenges with their Sexual and Reproductive Health and Rights (SRHRs) that are routinely swept under the carpet. This despite the fact that United National Population Fund states clearly that good sexual and reproductive health is an indispensable part of universal human rights and that it implies that people are able to have a satisfying and safe sex life, the capability to reproduce, and the freedom to decide if, when, and how often to do so.

Take the simplest aspect of menstrual health. How many schools provide adequate support, information and accessibility to menstrual health products?

Sunil Mehra, executive director of MAMTA, a Delhi-based non-profit working on adolescent and reproductive health issues says, "Our social and policy barriers do not allow the sexual and reproductive needs of adolescents (10 to 19 years) to be addressed because many of those who have sex are unmarried and below the age of consent."

There are other worrisome statistics. India has 253 million adolescents, more than any other country and equivalent to the combined populations of Japan, Germany and Spain, but the country is not doing enough to ensure that they become productive adults. A population council report says that, "No more than 20.3 per cent of unmarried boys and 8.2 per cent of unmarried girls used a condom consistently."

Spurred by concerns of HIV-AIDS, the Indian government in association with United Nations agencies introduced an adolescence-education programme (AEP) in 2005. Adolescent health featured for the first time as a national programme in 2006 under the National Adolescent Reproductive and Sexual Health Strategy (NARSHS), which included health clinics that offered preventive, promotive, curative and referral services for adolescents (10-19 years) and youth (19-24 years). Within two years of inception, the AEP was banned in 12 states, including Maharashtra, Karnataka, Kerala and Uttar Pradesh. The Madhya Pradesh chief minister found the illustrations too graphic; he wanted adolescent education focused on "yoga and Indian cultural values". The National Aids Control Organisation (NACO) removed contentious illustrations and words considered explicit, such as 'intercourse', 'condoms' and 'masturbate'.

In April 2009, a Rajya Sabha committee chaired by M Venkaiah Naidu, now Vice President of India and then member of Rajya Sabha (Upper House of Parliament), said the adolescent-education programme would "promote promiscuity of the worst kind, strike at the root of the cultural fabric, corrupt Indian youth and lead to the collapse of the education system and the decrease of virginity age."

The government has programmes, but the adults don't want to know and the teens do not know. Despite the fact that in October 2014, the government started the Rashtriya Kishor Swasthya Karyakram (RKSK) or National Adolescent Health Programme, independent studies reveal widespread ignorance. Reproductive health services ought to include counselling on menstrual disorders, menstrual hygiene, use of sanitary napkins, use of contraceptives, sexual concerns, sexual abuse and gender violence. While there has been a recent uptake in activities around menstrual hygiene and iron folic supplements through schools and immunization through anganwadi (day care centre) workers, sexual and reproductive health is "completely neglected."

The effort is now to engage adolescents through peer educators who would speak about various life skills, including nutrition, mental health, non-communicable diseases, gender and sexual and reproductive health. There is also the sensitizing of auxiliary nurse midwives, anganwadi workers, counsellors and medical officers to offer "non-judgmental services" for adolescent sexual and reproductive needs. Without sex education and counselling, adolescents are also at a high risk of acquiring sexually transmitted infections (STI) and even HIV.

In late January 2020, the Union Cabinet amended the 1971 Medical Termination of Pregnancy (MTP) Act allowing women to seek abortions as part of their reproductive rights and gender justice. The important amendment placed India in the top league of countries serving women who wish to make individual choices from their perspectives and predicaments."India will now stand amongst nations with a highly progressive law which allows legal abortions on a broad range of therapeutic, humanitarian and social grounds. It is a milestone which will further empower women, especially those who are vulnerable and victims of rape," Union Cabinet Minister for Textiles and Women and Child Development, Smriti Irani wrote on her blog.

Awareness and knowledge about SRHRs not just benefit the person, but also strengthen societies and nations. Schools are the perfect places to start with so as to achieve these health goals. A revised curriculum that addresses all aspects of human sexuality is the need of the hour. It ought to include information on biological processes, along with the emotional and psychological aspects involved. This alone is not enough. A proper orientation on consent, gender identity, interpersonal relationships need to happen. The final step would be to implement the curriculum across states. Where necessary, a contextualized sex-education would facilitate societal acceptance as also its effectiveness.

The digital era carries an inherent advantage of propagating verified and reliable information through online platforms. Comprehensive coverage of these issues in developed countries has helped young people make informed choices. The open conversations and progressive policies have helped normalize topics that have been considered 'taboo' and 'shameful' until now. Introducing these topics in a staggered manner from a young age reduces misconceptions and stigmas, especially regarding STDs, HIV/AIDS, sexuality spectrum (asexual, bisexuals, gays, lesbians, etc.), knowledge about contraceptive methods, and gender spectrum and many more.

With an upfront, wholesome and respectful sex/sexuality education, we empower people in their adolescent years. It is the right way to bolster self-identities and inculcate authentic individuality. Sex education moreover, nurtures a robust mental health among adolescents. The time is ripe to talk about emotions and feelings so that young people have permission to breathe and live their lives untainted by a sense of shame.

www.ingramcontent.com/pod-product-compliance
Lightning Source LLC
LaVergne TN
LVHW041148150826
845673LV00001B/96

9798896733010